M000202550

NOT A GOOD NEIGHBOR

NOT
A GOOD
NEIGHBOR

A Lawyer's Guide to Beating Big Insurance
by Settling Your Own Auto Accident Case

BRIAN LaBOVICK

LIONCREST
PUBLISHING

NOT A GOOD NEIGHBOR

*A Lawyer's Guide to Beating Big Insurance by
Settling Your Own Auto Accident Case*

ISBN   978-1-5445-1971-5 *Hardcover*

978-1-5445-1970-8 *Paperback*

978-1-5445-1969-2 *Ebook*

978-1-5445-1972-2 *Audiobook*

Every day, at some point, I have the opportunity
to throw salt over my shoulder.

It isn't superstition.

It is to remind me to be grateful for all my blessings.

Those blessings start with Esther and continue with our three children.

They are my inspiration.

Blaise Pascal's:
The Fulcrum
If +/something is
WORTH Believing
Why not Believe it.
Acceptance of
Fault
Concept of Free Will
Requires a
choice

C S Lewis/

Dr. John Lennox/

(Second Hand) (wine)

CONTENTS

INTRODUCTION

You've just had an automobile accident. You were moving innocently through a busy intersection when—BAM!—some clown runs a light and rams the back of your car.

Do you need a lawyer?

Maybe.

But maybe not.

You may be reading this and think, What? A lawyer telling me I don't need a lawyer? Isn't that like a doctor telling you to "walk it off" or a politician advising you to skip an election?

I'm sure skeptical people out there will say that if you ask a lawyer whether you need a lawyer, the answer is always yes! And that's probably a truthful statement. Most lawyers will tell you that you need to hire them if you want your auto accident handled in a way that protects your rights and ensures you get fair compensation. That's because lawyers are like other experienced professionals in that they can quickly see how to fix a problem. If you go to a surgeon to fix a medical problem, for example, chances are, you are going to be offered a surgical fix. That's what the surgeon knows. When I went with my daughter to the orthodontist, they not only showed me how terrible my daughter's bite was, but they also made me realize I needed braces, too!

But the fact is, in the legal world, especially in the car accident injury world, the majority of accidents do not need a lawyer. That is not to say that you can just sit back while the checks pour in from the insurance company to pay for all your suffering, expenses, and inconveniences. If you've been in a car wreck that wasn't your fault, you still need to take certain steps, investigate diligently, and negotiate carefully to ensure the insurance companies treat you fairly and honestly. You have to know how and when to seek medical treatment, and you have to understand how insurance policies are structured and how insurance adjusters work. You have to know your state laws about insurance coverage, and you certainly need to fully understand your own auto insurance policy and how to use it in case you have to. Most of all, you must recognize when the value of the claim is so high that the discount you will suffer doing the case alone will not be worth it and that you need to consult with a qualified injury lawyer to see if you can better maximize the case. Those cases are not as common as one may think. Most of the time, you can do this on your own.

There is a lot to know and remember, but you can do it—particularly if you're holding this book in your hands right now. In the chapters that follow, you'll find everything you need to navigate the process successfully. If the accident wasn't your fault, you can still negotiate a settlement with the other driver's insurance company and make as much as you would if you had a lawyer—but without having to pay the lawyer's percentage and costs.

DO I NEED A LAWYER?

With thousands of lawyers bombarding us on TV, billboards, radio, and internet ads, it seems like everyone needs a lawyer to handle every car accident case, right? How is it possible that most of us don't need lawyers?

What's more, how is it possible that one of those lawyers advertising about car accidents—me, for instance—is telling you that you don't need one?

Here's why: I want the cases where my client has significant, tragic, or catastrophic damages. Cases where people need surgery or have broken bones or a brain injury. Those are the types of cases that a nonlawyer will never get to full value on their own. The stakes are too high, and the insurance companies are far too crafty and experienced in cases like that for you to go it alone. You need an experienced hand to guide you, someone who understands all the insurance industry tricks and has a few tricks of their own. I will review some of those cases here, but my advice will be centered on understanding them and protecting your rights and not on handling that kind of complicated case on your own.

For all those other run-of-the-mill fender benders where drivers walk away with minor injuries, you're better off going it alone. All it takes is a little perseverance—and the advice found in this book.

GOING SOLO

I recently got a call from a man in Tampa named Surget, who was injured when a commercial pickup truck driver ran a red light and slammed into his Ford Edge in the middle of an intersection. The accident totaled Surget's vehicle. It sent him to the hospital with serious injuries.

Surget carried Florida's required personal injury protection insurance (PIP), which helped pay for his hospital bills, chiropractor visits, and MRI diagnostic exams. He made

State Farm/?

the claim on his own by calling the toll-free number on his insurance card. The operator he spoke to took his information and gave him a PIP claim number, and he used that for all his bills. It was fast and easy for him.

But Surget felt he needed some help dealing with the other driver's insurance company. He needed to get from point A—getting medical treatment for his injuries—to point B—getting a fair settlement from the other driver's insurance company. There seemed to be a lot of information, posturing, and evidence that needed to be developed before he could cross from point A to B, and he wasn't sure what the correct steps were. How would he go about getting a fair offer? What had to happen for that insurance company to say, "We want to give you X dollars to take care of you"? Surget did a great job providing the insurance companies the information they needed to evaluate his case. He even started the negotiation process, but it broke down because ✗ the adjuster was lowballing Surget on the offer to settle.

Surget was fortunate to call my office for help. I listened to what he'd done so far, and I was impressed with how smart and properly developed his case had become. So instead of taking him on as a client, I offered to coach him through the process. I explained that he needed to send the other driver's insurance company a more comprehensive demand ✓ letter, which is a formal offer to settle the case. I coached him on what he should say and what he should ask for in a way that would make sense to the adjuster. He wrote the letter and sent it off.

The other driver had a $100,000 policy limit. We asked them to tender their limits, and the company came back with an increased offer of $12,000, which was $9,000 more than their previous offer.

Surget countered with another demand, and they went back and forth with the negotiations until Surget got the offer up to $40,000. At that point, he called me back.

"I want you to take my case," he said. "I think we can get the full $100,000 limit!"

Surget was smart. He'd negotiated well, but he also knew that settlement offers often increase when you hire a lawyer.

I agreed that a lawyer could get him a higher offer from the insurance company. However, he was going to have a hard time getting the case to $100,000 with or without a lawyer. He was not getting any surgical intervention. His other value drivers were somewhat weak, and the property damage was not spectacular. It wasn't a bad case, but it was simply not a policy limits case without litigation. If we took his case into litigation, we could be offered the $100,000 near the trial date, but by that time, we would have incurred $20,000 in pretrial costs, which is the average amount it takes to prepare a case for court. When you do the math, it looks like this: The lawyer gets 40 percent of litigated case value; in this case, it would be around $40,000. In addition, the lawyer gets his investment back, which in this case would be the $20,000 pretrial costs. That means that $40,000 plus $20,000 is $60,000, and $60,000 minus $100,000 is $40,000! The adjuster recognized that Surget would get the same amount ($40,000) for settling early, just as he would if he hired an attorney and got the entire policy limits. In the end, the most he could hope to get was $40,000, and that payday might be two years away.

"Why don't you take your $40,000 now and skip the aggravation of litigation and the risk of a jury trial?" I said. Surget readily saw the logic. He took the $40,000 and was happy.

HOW TO PROTECT YOURSELF

Surget is an excellent example of why I'm writing this book.

Drivers like Surget who have been in an accident and find themselves negotiating with an insurance company can often negotiate their claims without hiring an attorney, saving time, money, and anxiety. To do that, however, those drivers need advice about how the system works and knowledge of how insurance companies think.

It is critical that you understand the process. It makes a big difference if you know how to best communicate with insurance companies—your own insurance company, as well as the other driver's insurers. What can you expect from them?

You need to know what you should do immediately after an accident to protect your rights. You must know where to get medical treatment that will help you recover, how to document your injuries for purposes of claim settlement, and how to build your case.

It is also wise to protect yourself before the accident ever happens. That's why you buy insurance, right? To make certain that when something bad happens, you are properly covered.

My law firm analyzed this and found that over 80 percent of our clients have no idea of what coverage is actually part of their insurance policy. Do you know how much coverage you have? Do you know what kind of insurance you carry? Do you know how much insurance is right for you? Do you know how different policies work together to cover your total losses?

Before you get into a bad situation, you should already have prepared yourself with proper levels of insurance. If you take the time to know what to purchase, you are less likely to need an attorney if you get hurt in a motor vehicle crash.

This book will help you sort through all of that. After thirty years as a personal injury attorney, I've probably seen all the mistakes victims can make in pursuing their cases after a motor vehicle accident. This book will help you avoid those mistakes while helping you decide if your case is significant enough to warrant the expense of hiring an attorney.

Surget was lucky because I was willing to chat on the phone and give him some free advice. Most attorneys won't do that, and quite honestly, when I'm busy with clients or in a trial, I don't have time to do that either. But Surget was a referral from a friend, and he caught me at a time when I was feeling generous. And the experience helped me realize that this book is needed for people who can get the job done without an attorney.

GETTING THE HELP YOU NEED

This book will give you all the advice you need to negotiate your settlement in many motor vehicle cases. I'll give you the tools to do this yourself. And if you do decide to hire an attorney, this book will help you better understand what they are doing for you and why.

Let's be clear about one thing: There are lots of situations when an injured motor vehicle accident victim needs an attorney. There are many car accident cases that are complicated. These include disputed liability cases, large policy limit cases where the injury is not being properly evaluated, or cases involving brain injuries that are exceptionally hard to quantify. Those cases typically need an attorney to get maximum value for the injured driver.

An attorney will also help you navigate the process. Many insurance companies are opaque, misleading, and ruthless, and this makes the path difficult for the average person. Insurance companies are profitable because they get you to buy as much coverage as possible and pay high premiums for years, then work to keep the claim payouts as low as possible. You may be on friendly terms with your insurance agent, but the insurance company your agent works for does not have your health and best interests in mind. Their sole interest is profit. Do not trust anyone who claims to be "The Good Hands People" or who declares that they're "On Your Side." Also, beware of geckos, cavemen, and claim reps named Flo. They are not your friends.

They are, however, very good at getting victims to accept less than they deserve.

My goal is not to teach you to be a lawyer. Instead, I want to make you aware of the pitfalls, help you save money, and protect yourself when you've been in a motor vehicle accident.

I'll fill you in on how an accident involving a commercial truck, railroad, or boat must be handled differently than an auto accident. No two accidents are the same. No state insurance laws are the same. Each policy is different.

For good measure, I'll also talk about other kinds of personal injury cases that almost always require an attorney, such as cases involving medical malpractice, product liability claims, and sexual harassment.

In the end, you'll be able to answer a simple question: Do I really need a lawyer?

Chances are, you don't.

CHAPTER ONE

ACTING FAST AFTER A CRASH

In the seconds following an automobile crash, you may not be thinking clearly. You might be in shock. You might have a concussion. Hell, you could be unconscious. Even if all you had was a minor fender bender, it's likely you'll be a bit frazzled.

That's why it's crucial that you take certain steps before the accident to ensure your rights and interests are adequately protected. Of course, take steps to protect yourself physically by wearing a seat belt, staying focused on your driving, ignoring the electronics and phones, and making sure your vehicle is in sound mechanical condition. Also, make sure your own insurance is adequate.

You also need to have the information and tools to document the accident ready and already stored in your car in case you are in an accident. These tools will allow you to quickly start gathering evidence to protect and maximize the value of your case.

Here's what you should carry: notepad, pen (or pencil if you live in a very cold area where a pen might freeze), a camera (if you don't have a smartphone), your proof-of-insurance card, and a copy of the checklist in Appendix A of this book. Pack these items in a sturdy ziplock bag so it's easy to find in a hurry. Elsewhere in your car, you should consider having a storage box that contains a flashlight with extra batteries, a road flare or two, jumper cables, a utility knife, and a blanket for trips in the wintertime.

In any accident that you can competently handle on your own and without an attorney, you will not be disabled by the accident. In a case where you are so hurt that you can't act right after an accident, you're likely to be more successful quickly hiring an attorney to document and maximize the injury value for you. But if you are not that badly hurt after an accident, then you need to take the steps necessary to start building your case immediately after the accident. This way, you will have the information and documentation you need to receive fair treatment from the insurance companies. What's vital for you to know is that car accidents are not only dangerous, but they are also expensive, and those who don't act quickly to protect their own interests can easily get steamrollered by the at-fault driver and their heartless insurance company.

Here's an example: I had one client who was stopped at a four-way stop. When it was his turn to go, he proceeded through the intersection. But just as he was accelerating, a driver to his right ran the stop sign, and my client plowed into him.

My client was knocked unconscious and woke up in the hospital. Two hours later, a policeman showed up. He asked my client how he was feeling.

"I feel like I was hit by a truck," he said.

He thought the cop might laugh, but he didn't.

"I'm sorry," the cop said, "but I have to give you a ticket."

My client was still collecting his thoughts, but he was aware enough to react immediately.

"What?" he said. "Why am I getting a ticket? The other guy ran the stop sign, not me."

The cop told him that the other driver gave him a different story. The other driver claimed he stopped at the stop sign and that the collision occurred when my client ran the stop sign. What's more, the other driver had a passenger with him, and they both claimed my client was at fault.

It's your word against the word of two other people. What do you do in a situation like that?

In that case, the injured driver decided not to pursue his case alone and hired me to help. This was a wise choice because he was hospitalized and unable to do the immediate legwork needed to collect evidence that would refute the other driver's lies. For example, during our investigation, we located a video camera at a nearby gas station. Luckily, the camera was trained on the intersection, and the video taken the day of the accident hadn't yet been erased or taped over. When we reviewed the video, it was clear that the other driver and his passenger were lying.

The first thing we did was fight the ticket the cop gave my client. We used the video in court to show that my client hadn't broken any traffic laws but that the other driver had. We wanted to make sure my client didn't have anything on their driving record that provided ammunition for the other driver's insurance company to deny my client's claim.

The second thing we did was to show the video to the other driver's insurance company. The fact that the other driver's lie made life very difficult for my client was a factor we cited in preparing our demand letter to that company.

Let me pause here for a strategy break. There are some good reasons you would want to show this video to the insurance company and win the liability argument in the "presuit" negotiations phase (we call this phase "presuit" because it is the time period before we file a lawsuit), especially if you do not want to litigate your case. You can't litigate without an attorney. If you want to litigate this kind of case, you will need to consult with your lawyer before disclosing such significant impeachment material. Your lawyer may have a strategy that allows the other side to go under oath and testify as to the facts and circumstances before disclosing this damaging video evidence they have to the contrary. Just think about it before giving up any really damaging evidence that proves a disputed point. It may help you get a settlement presuit, but make sure that is what you want.

In this case, my client was able to get a substantial settlement of around $225,000. The at-fault driver's lie caused the adjuster to lose faith in him, and I believe that drove up the value of the settlement by $50,000 to $75,000. If we had gone to trial, where I would have been able to show the at-fault driver's bad behavior, I would have asked for at least $500,000. But my client was not interested in going to court.

The moral of the story is that when you're in a motor vehicle accident, everyone is looking out for themselves, and people may not tell the truth about what happened. People who have been in an accident will automatically try to defend their own actions and try to deflect blame. Even those who are not outright lying can also be uncertain about the facts. People often perceive things differently; what you think happened may be dramatically different from what someone else believes happened.

If you've ever seen the acclaimed 1950 film *Rashomon*, you know what I'm talking about. *Rashomon*, directed by the famed Akira Kurosawa, involves various characters in a court telling subjective, self-serving, and wildly varying versions of the same incident—the death of a samurai and the rape of his wife in eighth-century Japan. Each witness tells a different story, but each witness seems to be telling the truth, and their tale is perfectly plausible. The film gave rise to a term, the Rashomon effect, which describes how eyewitness recollections of the same event are often contradictory and unreliable.

The same thing happens after a motor vehicle accident.

As a result of this Rashomon effect, it's imperative that you don't accept everything people claim and that you avoid admitting fault until you've had time to think through what happened and collect any outside information that is available to you.

AFTER THE ACCIDENT

If you're in a motor vehicle accident, the first thing you must do is assess your injuries and get help if you need it.

But if you aren't hurt or if your injuries seem minor, there are things you can do at the accident scene. First, you must try to figure out exactly what happened. Think back to what you were doing before the accident happened. Be clear in your mind about what occurred before you ask the other person what happened. Many times, the guilty party will admit their mistake before the police arrive and accept fault because that's how many people are raised—to take responsibility for their errors and not lie. If you can get the other driver to admit their mistake and you can document that, it will save you a lot of time later when the police and insurance companies are trying to assign blame.

(Strategy hint: You attract more bees with honey than with vinegar. If you get out of your car and start shouting, the other party will clam up and not admit anything. If you get out of your car and ask if the other party is okay and then kindly ask why they hit you, many times you will get back, "I am sorry. I don't know what I was thinking." Or, "I looked down at my radio, and the traffic stopped in front of me. I didn't look up in time." Or even better: "I was dialing my phone, and when I looked up, it was too late." When the police do arrive on the scene, you can calmly explain to the officer that the other driver already apologized to you and admitted fault.

After you get your admission, you should document the accident scene as best you can. Grab the toolkit from your glove box. Smartphones are perfect for documenting evidence. Take photos and video. Talk to witnesses and get their names and contact information. If anyone has suffered injuries, take photos. Take photos of the people at the scene as well as the cars. If there's an intersection light and the other driver hasn't admitted fault, take video and pictures of the intersection's light sequence. Make notes of everything in the vicinity—businesses, road markings, signs, crosswalks. If you had a passenger with you, ask them to help if they are able. If the other side has a passenger, ask if they are okay and then ask what they saw. Many times, the passenger was reading or sleeping or looking out the window. Many people won't want to be involved, but they know the person they were driving with was at fault, so they say they were not watching. If you can get them to commit to whatever they saw, they are less likely to be a witness against you later. People don't realize how powerful an admission is in court. The admission of the driver, your opponent in a lawsuit, is permitted evidence in court. The passenger's statements could be admissible as an excited utterance. So try to get it early on after you get out of the car. A lot of good things happen when you can start documenting the accident right from the start.

This could make you uncomfortable, and it may seem undignified to some people. But most would be surprised to learn how many times victims have protected their rights by having the wherewithal to take pictures and collect evidence at the scene of an accident. There is nothing unsavory or crass about documenting what happened to you. You not only have the right but an obligation to protect your interests.

You will want to know the name of everyone who was at the scene of your accident, particularly anyone who would be a good witness. You want to know who these people are because the other driver's lawyers are going to know it, and they are going to track them down. You want to get to them first. The more people you get to first, the better. You want to get their names, cell phone numbers, and email addresses. Get a statement from them if you can. If you can't get a statement, get a general idea from them of what they remember. You can get a witness statement from them later.

If you act quickly after an accident, you will be ahead of the insurance company. You will put yourself in a more powerful position later when you are negotiating a settlement. People's memories change over time, so you want to get their statements while the events are still fresh in their minds. Video files, like the one I located at the gas station, are lost or recorded over, so you want to secure them as quickly as possible. You want to ask the police officer on the scene to check the sequence timing of the traffic light to make sure both drivers didn't have simultaneous green lights that caused them to collide.

DO I NEED A LAWYER?

When deciding whether you need a lawyer, you have to ask yourself how much work like this you're willing to do on your case and how difficult it will be for you to get the right information. In the previous case, where my client woke up in the hospital, would my client have thought to check for video from the gas station near his accident site? Would the gas station manager have been willing to give him access to the video the way they granted us access?

I don't know.

I do know that when our office does an investigation, we pull computer records on everyone involved. We learn how many insurance claims our client has made and how many claims the other driver has made. We send out questionnaires to all the witnesses, and a lot of times, we call them ahead of time and get an interview before they even fill out the questionnaire. If it's a big case, we'll hire a court reporter for that interview and videotape it as well.

We get photos of all the property damage. We get detailed

repair estimates for all the vehicles involved. The insurance company will look at a $3,000 repair and say the damage was minor. But we'll notice that $1,200 of the bill was for straightening the frame of a Ford F-150 pickup, and we'll use that to show the force of the impact. It takes quite a blow to bend the frame of an F-150. Is our client going to develop long-term neck injuries as a result of that kind of impact?

All of these details are crucial toward developing a powerful settlement letter, also called a demand letter for the insurance company. Some people may not be willing to spend the time and effort to gather all this data. Those people should consider getting some legal help.

But if you're comfortable drilling down into your own case and doing all the legwork that's required, you can save yourself a lot of money and resolve your case faster. What I have noticed is that many people are really smart about their case. They know the details better than anyone. Those details make a big difference. Write them down and get ready to use them in the demand letter. Each small point can build on other small points to make a powerful impact on the opposing adjuster.

LOOK OUT FOR YOURSELF

A lot of drivers mistakenly think the responding police

officer will document the facts of the accident well. Some officers who respond are specially trained traffic officers, and if the accident is severe, the police might send out an accident reconstruction specialist or a homicide officer. But for your garden-variety traffic accident, the responding officer is going to ask each party what happened, and if they both claim it was the other guy's fault, the officer will file a report that says no one is at fault. He'll let the two drivers go figure it out in civil court.

You can't kick back and expect the officer to do your legwork for you. In many courts, an investigation and accident report can't be evidence. In some states, the testimony taken by the officer at the scene is considered privileged and can't be used as evidence. For example, if the officer records that the other driver admitted to being distracted by their phone before the crash, your attorney can't later confront the other driver about that statement in court. It helps to have that information, but it's no guarantee that the facts are now perfectly documented for your use later in your accident claim.

You need to be looking out for yourself.

I had one client who did a particularly good job of this. Their case wasn't an auto accident; it occurred on another kind of vehicle—a cruise ship.

Our client was a fifty-eight-year-old woman on a cruise with her boyfriend, a retired trial lawyer. Our client was walking down the stairs to a gala banquet when the heel of her stiletto shoe got stuck in a small gap in the tile on the steps. The gap wasn't obvious, but it was big enough to catch the client's heel. When she went to take another step, her shoe came off, causing her to tumble to the bottom of the stairs. It was a bad fall.

The boyfriend rushed down to help her. When he looked back up the stairs, he saw her shoe hanging there, the heel still wedged in the crack. He pulled out his phone and took a photo of the shoe up on the stairs. Then, while she was sitting at the bottom of the steps being treated by a crew member, he bounded back up the stairs and took close-up photos showing the shoe's heel in the crack.

The cruise company insisted their stairs hadn't caused that fall. She must have tripped and fallen on her own, they said, and declined to take responsibility.

Then we showed them the photos.

Suddenly, the conversation changed.

Are you sure you don't want to pay this poor woman something? Or should we just sue you and let a jury take a look at these photos?

Eventually, we did sue. You almost always have to sue cruise lines because they are self-insured and rarely settle anything until a lawsuit is filed. Eventually, we settled the case for $150,000.

THE IMPORTANCE OF PHOTOS

Pictures are valuable because people's memories are unreliable. Pictures sharpen an accident victim's memory. Photos can also help defendants better understand what happened and what their culpability is.

We've had photos and video work against our cases, too. For example, we had another client on a cruise ship who sat down to lunch on the lido deck. His chair was one of those plastic stackable chairs, and when he sat in it, one of the legs broke, and he landed on the deck and herniated a disk in his back.

At least that's what he told us happened.

The cruise line had a video of the area, and when we reviewed the video, it became clear that the chair leg hadn't broken at all. It had bowed somewhat, but our client had jumped to his feet to prevent a fall. He didn't look injured at all.

That video was very telling about my client and his poor recollection of what happened. And it undermined his entire case because it made it appear as though he'd been lying. Had the bowed leg caused him to injure his back? Maybe. But the video made it difficult for anyone to believe that this incident injured my client significantly. This hurt his case dramatically. Now, if I'd been aware of the video ahead of time, we might have been able to work with it. Perhaps the bowing of the leg and his sudden jump to his feet was enough to cause the injury. But that option disappeared when the video completely contradicted my client's recollection of what happened.

WHO'S GOING TO PAY FOR ALL THIS?

Most drivers face a torrent of questions after they've been in a motor vehicle accident that wasn't their fault. Who is going to pay for my medical bills? Who's going to pay for my car repair? Can I get a rental car? Who is going to pay for the rental car? What if I have to stay home and can't work? Who is going to pay for my lost wages? If the other driver is at fault, what kind of help can I expect from my insurance company?

Let's cover property damage issues first.

PROPERTY DAMAGE

If you have auto insurance and your car is damaged in an

accident that wasn't your fault, you have a choice as to whose insurance to use. You can use your own insurance because it's a no-fault insurance and will cover the damages to your car even if you were negligent. This coverage is called comprehensive and collision coverage. It covers your car's damages (collision) and the stuff in and around your car (comprehensive). It usually has a deductible of $500, $1,000, or $2,000. You are required to pay that deductible when you are at fault in causing the damages to your own car.

But when someone else is responsible for causing damage to your car, there are ways to avoid paying that deductible. If the at-fault driver has decent insurance, it will include "property damage" coverage. This pays for any property damages—including damage to your car—that the driver causes.

So there are now two policies covering the same damages, and the two adjusters usually work out the repairs quickly between each other. They use the accident report and telephone statements from the drivers to determine fault. The at-fault driver's adjuster will use their client's property damage to cover the other driver's car damage claim or your adjuster will use your comp and collision to cover your claim—with the understanding that the at-fault driver's policy will pay the deductible. Once your adjuster pays a claim on your car, you assign them the right to go after the other guy's insurance for the damages paid.

Allowing the two adjusters to work this out while your car gets repaired is the easiest path to getting your car fixed. Your evidence of the other driver's culpability can help you get your claim quickly covered without paying the deductible. If fault is disputed, give your adjuster your account of the accident and any evidence showing the other driver is at fault. Every insurance policy requires policyholders to cooperate with the insurance company's investigation; you must report the accident quickly and give a statement to your own company when asked.

When it comes to working with adjusters, your experience may vary. Some adjusters will say, "We'll pay it all. Let us worry about it." Others will say, "Look, you pay for the repair and the deductible under your own collision policy, and if I can get the deductible back from the other guy's property damage insurance, I'll send you a check." The worst companies will say, "If you want your deductible back, sue for your money. I am not helping. I am getting your car fixed, and you are paying your deductible, and I am closing my file."

If you have comp and collision, your insurance company should never leave it to you to handle. Your company should be getting this damage paid for you. That's what you pay them a big premium to do.

That said, it's sometimes easier to call the other driver's insurance company—especially if you have a clear liability issue—and ask the adjuster to cover your loss. Many adjusters will accept 100 percent fault and pay the repair shop. Sometimes they will agree to pay for a rental car. You may also have rental car coverage on your own policy; it's inexpensive coverage and a wonderful benefit, especially if the repair shop has a rental agency as many large dealerships have.

Taking your car to a preauthorized shop will also save you time and effort in getting the property damage handled quickly. All major insurance companies have preauthorized repair shops that have a direct connection to the insurance company and a good relationship with the adjusters. Dealer repair shops and quality local shops usually have these relationships in place.

Nevertheless, it's important to be cautious when working with preauthorized shops. Many of these shops will give you a preliminary estimate that details the damages they can see. This estimate will specifically disclaim any underlying damages they can't see. Using the preliminary estimate, your adjuster may say, "The estimate of damages is $2,300. Your deductible is $500. Do you want a check for

$1,800, or do you want to go forward with the repairs and pay the deductible?"

Unless you are planning on getting rid of the car, do not take the money. This preliminary estimate is intentionally low, and if you approve the repairs, the repair shop will take the car apart, and most times, lo and behold, they find more damage. A supplemental damage bill then must be submitted and paid by your insurance company.

Why do the repair shops even bother with superficial preliminary estates? Because many people will take the cash and continue to drive the damaged car. They don't mind having a dented bumper or a scratched side panel. The insurance company knows this, so many times they can settle a claim without having to spend more to fully repair the vehicle. This saves the insurance company thousands of dollars each time it happens and millions of dollars a year. The company takes advantage of a person's greed or need for money and gets out of paying the full value of what they contracted to cover. I'm convinced repair shops agree to give these low-ball preliminary estimates in return for becoming a preauthorized shop.

As you can tell, there is a lot more to dealing with insurance companies than most people realize. And learning how to deal with them starts before you even slide behind the wheel. It starts with buying an insurance policy that protects you, and there are a lot of confusing options out there. Read on to find out how to choose a policy that is right for you.

___

CHAPTER TWO

UNDERSTANDING MOTOR VEHICLE INSURANCE

The first step to protecting yourself from a debilitating long-term injury in the event of an accident that isn't your fault is to make sure your own policy covers you adequately.

When shopping for insurance, you must find out what your state's minimum requirements are. Each state has different requirements, and these requirements will determine how much you pay for insurance in your state. My home state of Florida, for example, requires you to carry $10,000 in personal injury protection (PIP) and $10,000 in property damage insurance. The PIP coverage is for your medical bills, and the property damage insurance is used when you're at fault and must pay for the other driver's car and property damages.

Those $10,000 levels are the bare minimum. If you have an accident with this level of coverage, your insurance is only obligated to pay medical bills up to $10,000 and property damage up to $10,000. If your injuries are severe, or if you totaled the other driver's $75,000 Tesla, you're on the hook for expenses over those minimum levels. Your health insurance, if you have it, will help you with your medical bills after your PIP runs out, but you have no backstop for property damages. The Tesla driver can sue you for the $65,000 he needs to replace the car you damaged.

Smart drivers purchase coverage beyond their state minimums. They want to make sure that if they hurt someone and get sued, their policy will provide their legal defense and enough money to settle the case. These drivers understand that they need to protect themselves to the tune of hundreds of thousands of dollars because people driving vehicles can hurt each other to the tune of hundreds of thousands of dollars or even millions of dollars. All it takes is a simple mistake. You're driving down the highway, and a bee flies through the window and stings you on the ear, and you slam into the truck in front of you, which lurches forward and strikes three pedestrians in a crosswalk, and now you're being sued for $20 million (crazy but true).

Driving a car is dangerous. We should insure ourselves well for it, but most people don't.

TYPES OF AUTO INSURANCE

Car insurance related to liability coverage comes in two basic flavors. The first is a policy typically used in a commercial environment. It has one number that covers every loss in an accident, and the policy limits are often high. For example, if the policy limit is $1 million, it would cover the vehicle owner, the vehicles, and any person hurt by that vehicle. This includes any bodily injury, property damage, lost wages, medical bills, or anything else someone could sue you for up to $1 million. A lot of commercial trucks have $2 million or $5 million policies that cover everything. That is commonly called a CSL or combined single limit policy. It is not the typical policy one finds in a collision between two drivers.

The second flavor of injury liability insurance is a personal policy with a lower number first and a higher number second. For instance, a typical policy would show coverage for bodily injury liability 100/300 or 50/100 or some other combination of numbers. The first number indicates what your policy limits are for each *person* involved in your accident. The second number indicates the *total coverage for all the people* hurt in your accident. So if your policy limit for bodily injury liability is 100/300, that means your policy will pay $100,000 for each person you injure, up to a total of $300,000. If you injure five people, they would have to split the $300,000 five ways. If there are only two people, then the most the policy would pay is $200,000.

I tell my clients that 100/300 for bodily injury liability is bare bones. That's the absolute minimum you want to carry. I advise most of my clients to carry 250/500 or 300/500 or whatever your insurance offers. Some offer 300/500, and others offer 300/600. It just depends on the company.

UMBRELLA COVERAGE

The higher levels protect you better if you cause an accident. That improved coverage also allows you to go to your homeowner insurance company and ask for an umbrella policy. Let me explain why improved homeowners insurance helps you if you have a severe auto accident.

Homeowners insurance typically covers your losses if your house burns down, your dog bites someone, or a guest falls into a sinkhole in your backyard and sues you. An umbrella policy will cover you for almost anything that causes you to be sued, except for intentional acts such as battery or sexual harassment. If you cause a serious auto accident and the damages exceed your auto coverage, an umbrella policy can provide additional coverage and keep you out of bankruptcy. This umbrella insurance is supplemental to the regular homeowner's policy and needs to be paid for separately.

However, to qualify for an umbrella policy for your homeowner's policy, your homeowner's insurance company will require that you carry a high level of car insurance, such as 250/500 bodily injury liability coverage. That's because the homeowner's insurance company does not want you to use your umbrella coverage in auto accidents except under extraordinary conditions. The homeowner's insurance company wants the automobile insurance company to handle 99 percent of all your automobile accident claims, and the way they can make sure that happens is to force you to have a lot of automobile insurance coverage.

The beauty of an umbrella policy is that the additional coverage you get is a lot cheaper than if you were to add that additional coverage to your auto insurance. For example, if you are paying $1,000 every six months for a 250/500 on your auto insurance, the cost could double if you want to increase your bodily injury liability to 500/1,000 ($500,000 per person and $1 million per accident). However, if you keep your auto insurance at 250/500, you can qualify for a homeowner's umbrella policy of $1 million for much less—something on the order of $300 a year for $1 million of umbrella coverage. If you want far better insurance coverage, it's cheaper to add an umbrella policy than to increase your auto insurance.

There are many advantages to carrying a higher level of insurance. The amount of money you stand to lose in an injury accident can be extraordinary. People don't realize how quickly the money goes and how staggering the expenses can be.

Most people think $100,000 is a huge amount of money. It's a life-altering sum for most people. However, it's not a large sum in an injury case, where a single surgery can cost $150,000 and the cost for therapy, future surgeries, hospital bills, prescriptions, legal bills, and lost wages can add even more mind-blowing amounts.

If you are carrying the bare minimum of $100,000 per person and $300,000 per accident and you're at fault in a bad auto accident, you could wind up with a huge legal judgment on your head. And the only way to get out from under that is through bankruptcy.

UNINSURED MOTORISTS

In addition to protecting yourself when you cause an accident, you also have to protect yourself when an at-fault driver carries insufficient insurance to cover the damages they cause you to suffer. This type of insurance is called uninsured motorist (UM) or underinsured motorist (UIM) coverage, and it's the flip side of bodily injury insurance.

Most states require that you first get bodily injury (BI) coverage before you can purchase UM/UIM. Then you need to ask your automobile insurance agent to add UM/UIM to your policy. Once you have both BI and UM/UIM, you can also call your homeowner's insurance agent and add a UM/UIM rider on top of the umbrella policy if you decide to get that.

Each state treats UM and UIM differently. Some make it stackable, so it pays off in addition to other coverages. Some states make UM/UIM only apply *above* what the other party has, and other states make UM/UIM apply *instead of* what the other party has in coverage. My state, Florida, makes it easy. UM and UIM are the same, which means it does not matter if the other driver is totally uninsured or just underinsured. Both UM and UIM are simply in addition to whatever the defendant has in total coverage. If an at-fault driver has $10,000 of BI coverage, and my client has $100,000 in UM/UIM coverage, then the total coverage, in this case, would be $110,000. In Florida, any damages you suffer in excess of the at-fault driver's $10,000 BI coverage would be covered by your UM/UIM coverage.

UM/UIM coverage is confusing and tricky. For example, in Florida, if you settle the BI case against the at-fault driver, you must first tell your UM/UIM carrier. If you don't tell them you are taking money from the BI carrier, you can lose your rights to money from your UM/UIM carrier. That is a harsh outcome for not knowing the rules. Your UM/UIM carrier has this right because in Florida, your UM/UIM carrier is allowed to sue the person who caused the damages that your UM/UIM carrier paid to you. The UM/UIM carrier can sue the defendant to get that money back. This does not happen often. Usually, the UM/UIM carrier, once told by the plaintiff that the BI carrier is tendering their policy limits, will waive their rights and let the BI carrier pay the plaintiff directly. But you still must ask because sometimes the UM/UIM carrier knows the defendant is very rich, and they can collect against the defendant. In those cases, the UM/UIM carrier will actually give you the BI settlement money and then sue the defendant to get it back. They will also sue the defendant for any money they must pay you on your UM/UIM coverage. So you can see why I call it tricky.

Still, it is much better to have UM/UIM. When you call your homeowner's insurance agent about the umbrella policy, ask them to give you a UIM or UM rider on the homeowner's policy as well. With that rider, not only are you covered by your $250,000 BI liability but also by the $1 million umbrella policy you bought for the rest of the world.

BUYING THE RIGHT INSURANCE

Auto insurance is a fact of life for most people. Even if

you never get in an accident or file a claim, it's crucial that you buy the right insurance. Having the right policy gives you some peace of mind and at least some reassurance that if you do have an accident, you won't have to file for bankruptcy.

What are the basic components for insurance, and how much coverage do you need? Here's a quick overview.

PERSONAL INJURY PROTECTION

When shopping for insurance, the first thing you need to know is what your state minimum requirements are. For example, some states require that you carry insurance that will help you pay your medical bills resulting from an accident, regardless of whether you are at fault. This coverage is called personal injury protection (PIP), and twelve states require that you carry it, although the levels vary by state.

PIP insurance is also known as no-fault insurance because payouts are not determined by who is responsible. Even when you're not at fault, your PIP insurance can be tapped to cover your medical bills and work loss and those of your passengers. If your state doesn't require PIP, you might still consider carrying it if your comprehensive health insurance is limited. By the same token, if you have great health insurance, PIP is less essential. Some states don't have PIP, even for voluntary purchase, and in those states, I suggest buying the additional medical payments insurance for additional medical coverage.

PIP can cover everything from medical and surgical treatment to ambulance fees and rehabilitation, up to the limits of the policy. PIP, like almost all the components of auto insurance, varies in benefits and coverage according to which state you are in. In Florida, for instance, PIP insurance covers 80 percent of your medical bills and 60 percent of your lost wages up to $10,000.

Even among the twelve states that require PIP, the cost varies wildly. In Florida, the average premium is around $200 a month, whereas in North Dakota, it's $45. Michigan is the real outlier, though; PIP premiums there are about $628 a month because until recently, the state required drivers to carry unlimited PIP. People injured in Michigan could expect a smorgasbord of benefits, from in-home nursing care to specialized medical treatments. The state has since lowered its minimum required PIP coverage in an effort to reduce its highest-in-the-nation auto insurance policies. For example, if you are a Medicaid recipient, you can reduce your PIP coverage to $50,000. If you're on Medicare and your health insurance covers car accident injuries, you can even opt out of PIP altogether.

BODILY INJURY LIABILITY

As we mentioned earlier, bodily injury liability (called BI or BIL) is the most important and expensive element of your auto insurance policy. It covers the medical costs for people you injure when an accident is your fault. It doesn't cover your own injuries or expenses, but it can be a buffer when the accident is particularly bad.

BIL coverage also ensures you get a lawyer to defend you, and it pays to settle that case for one person or a group of people. I strongly suggest a minimum of 100/300 in BI, which is $100,000 per person and $300,000 incident.

Sometimes your policy liability limits are listed with three numbers, such as 30/60/15. When you see that, the third number represents the limit on the coverage for property damage, including cars, buildings, or other nonhuman losses. Other policies list property damage liability as a separate component.

Some states don't require BI, and many people don't carry it. It's a calculated risk; these people figure that if they cause an accident, the other guy won't be able to collect from them because they don't have any money and drive a beater car. In Florida, the bet is a good one. It is hard to collect against underinsured people. The debtor laws in Florida protect people who owe money. Not having insurance, when you are uncollectible, isn't such a terrible option. Of course, if you are uninsured and you are hurt by someone who is uninsured, then you are both out of luck.

In states that require BIL, the level of coverage varies. Louisiana requires BIL of $15,000 per person, whereas Maine requires $50,000. Florida doesn't require any BIL, and neither does New Jersey. Most states that mandate BIL coverage have a minimum coverage level of $25,000.

But those minimum levels are insufficient to cover damages in many accidents. If you own a home, have some savings, or possess other assets that could be lost in a lawsuit, $25,000 in BIL coverage is inadequate. If you cause an accident that injures someone badly, that policy limit could be met quickly, and the person you hurt could sue you for the expenses they've incurred as a result of your poor driving.

As I mentioned previously, the best route to take is to get your BIL coverage high enough so that you qualify for an umbrella policy through your homeowner's insurance. That umbrella policy covers you no matter where the accident occurs—your home, your boat, your car—but you can't get one unless you're carrying a minimum level of homeowner's and BIL coverage. Your auto policy's BIL typically must be 250,000/500,000 before your insurance company will give you an umbrella policy. Umbrella coverage is cheap. I pay $50 per month for $4 million in extra coverage.

PROPERTY DAMAGE LIABILITY

This coverage, which we discussed earlier in this chapter, protects you if you harm another person's property.

There are a lot of expensive cars on the road today, so I recommend people carry about $50,000 in property damage coverage. The cost of upgrading from $10,000 to $50,000 is not that much. Even $50,000 doesn't sound like a lot, as there are basic trucks now that are more than $50,000. Still, property damage is not the thing that will sink your financial battleship. Human injury and damages are what can really mess you up. Fifty-thousand dollars is typically sufficient in the cases I've seen.

For comprehensive and collision insurance, get the minimum of your agent prices. I suggest a $500 deductible. It will be more expensive than a $1,000 deductible, but not by a lot. A $1,000 or $2,000 deductible is okay, too, but I feel like the premium savings isn't enough to make the out-of-pocket expense worth it if you really do crash your car.

UNINSURED OR UNDERINSURED MOTORISTS

Although all states except New Hampshire (Live Free or Die) require drivers to carry some amount of auto insurance, the Insurance Information Institute reports that about 13 percent of all drivers don't carry any insurance. Some people don't think insurance is important. Others don't have a policy because they can't afford it. This is often the case with drivers whose insurance rates are astronomical because they have such a terrible driving record—precisely the type of individual who should be carrying insurance.

States have struggled to root out uninsured drivers, and many states have gone after them in novel ways. Many states penalize uninsured drivers who get caught—fines can be as high as $5,000, and some drivers get their licenses revoked or their cars impounded. Some go to jail.

Other states go after uninsured motorists with "no pay, no play" laws that prevent uninsured motorists from suing for pain and suffering if they've been hurt in an accident caused by someone else. Missouri has this law, although that state will allow an uninsured motorist to sue if the at-fault driver was driving under the influence or was convicted of manslaughter or second-degree murder. California and Michigan also limit uninsured motorists' rights to sue. Don't get the idea that when there is a manslaughter charge involved, you should handle your own claim. This is clearly a situation when hiring counsel is best.

Still, the number of uninsured motorists remains high, and the best solution has been to put the onus on responsible drivers by mandating they carry uninsured motorist insurance coverage (UM). Twenty-two states require that drivers carry uninsured motorist coverage, and fourteen require underinsured motorist coverage (UIM). UM compensates policyholders when the at-fault driver either has no liability insurance or fled the accident scene without being identified. UIM covers drivers when the offending driver carries insufficient liability coverage to adequately cover the damage they caused.

UM covers only you when you're injured in the accident, and your comprehensive and collision coverage will cover your car and other property damage. In some states, insurance agents offer both comp and collision and UIM property damage. If my policy has both of those listed, I would ask my agent what the difference is and ask whether the coverage is redundant.

How much UIM coverage should you carry? You know how much I like umbrella policies, but if you have a limited budget and need to make your automobile insurance as affordable as possible, I recommend my clients carry the same level of UM/UIM insurance for themselves as they carry in BIL coverage. Your health is just as important as the health of another driver, right? Other factors to consider are how much your state requires you to carry and what other means you might have to pay for your medical bills in the event of an accident. PIP, if it's required in your state, will cover your medical bills up to a certain point. But if you're badly injured in a hit-and-run accident, you may feel fortunate to have plenty of UM coverage.

WHAT YOU'LL PAY FOR INSURANCE

Insurance companies use something called an insurance score to determine how much you'll pay for your policy. An insurance score is essentially a computer-generated prediction of how likely you are to file an insurance claim. It's much like your credit score. Your insurance score takes into account your amount of debt, the length of your credit history, your payment history, the amount of revolving credit you have versus the amount of credit in the form of loans, how much credit is available to you, and your monthly account balances.

Ironically, your insurance score doesn't take into account your income, so you can be penalized by taking out a large loan, even if your income will cover the payments easily.

Insurance scores are part of an opaque process that varies by company, but the insurance industry stands by them because it feels there is a strong correlation between your credit score and insurance claims. I guess one way to look at it is that people with poor credit are more likely to file more claims because they don't have the money to make repairs on their damaged vehicles. It's nearly impossible to qualify for a company's lowest possible rate. According to Investopedia, you can have a credit score in the high 700s, own your home, and have no balances on your credit cards and still not earn that low rate.

And here's another irony: You can have a flawless driving

record and still pay more than someone with a spotty driving record if your credit score is lower than the poor driver's score. Other factors that affect your insurance rates are your age, where you live, the type of car you drive, your driving record, and your race. The rate you pay is not negotiable; if you don't like the price, they'll probably suggest you go talk to Geico. The only way to avoid high rates is to have a great driving record, a great credit score, and children who ride bicycles until they're in their late twenties. That's because young people are more likely to get into a wreck than experienced drivers. The damages associated with that wreck will be paid by the person driving and the car's owner. It can also be held against the parents in some states. In Florida, for example, any person under eighteen years old must have a parent or guardian sign off that they will be responsible for everything that child does in a car. So if your son or daughter borrows a neighbor's car and crashes it, the parent who signed the permission form for the state is personally responsible for those damages. Other states have similar laws. Insurance is expensive for young drivers, and parents must pay for it or require their child to wait till they are eighteen to get a driver's license. Then they can drive their own car with their own insurance.

Other than the rates they charge, there are other ways to evaluate which insurance company you buy your policy from. There are many different rating systems, including ones from Moody's and *Consumer Reports*, and what you look for are high scores in things such as customer service, easy procedures, speed of action, and rental car arrangements. For instance, some companies have a deal with Enterprise that allows their customers who need a car while theirs is being repaired to simply give the rental agency a claim number, and they'll give you a car at no charge. The expense just becomes part of your claim.

Things like that make it easier to choose an auto insurance carrier. But the real question for most consumers should be, who pays it off? Who treats their clients fairly? When you consider that, the list of appealing insurance companies gets short quickly. "The Good Hands People"? They'll slap you around with those hands. The clever gecko? He's a sweetheart on TV, but he's a real lizard as a claims adjuster.

But there are some good companies out there. My experience is that Chubb Insurance out of New York is exceptional. We are Farmers dum de dum dum dum! is a good company, although it used to be better when they were smaller. USAA is another good company most of the time. I have known many State Farm adjusters, and they were pretty good at adjusting their clients' claims.

To give you an idea of how big these insurance companies are and how much money they make, consider what happened in 1992. That's the year Hurricane Andrew hit the Bahamas, Florida, and Louisiana, Hurricane Iniki clobbered Hawaii, and farmers in the Midwest were wiped out by massive floods. Insurance claims from these disasters were astronomical. Hurricane Andrew alone did almost $30 billion in damage. Yet, State Farm came out of that disastrous year with huge profits. In what had to have been the worst natural-disaster year in their history, I believe State Farm managed to pocket about a third of a billion dollars. According to a company press release, the State Farm group ended 2019 with a net worth of $100.9 billion.

You read that correctly.

Net worth: OVER A HUNDRED BILLION DOLLARS.

That just gives you an idea of how much money these companies make.

COORDINATING DIFFERENT INSURANCES

Each state has a scheme that sets out which insurance policy pays first and which policies follow. In almost all states, workers' comp pays first. If you are injured on the job, even while driving on the job, your workers' compensation should cover your losses. You will need to go to your supervisor and report the accident and injury to get that started.

We handle workers' compensation at our firm, but that is the topic of another book! If you are not working, then workers' compensation is not applicable. Your automobile insurance is the primary, or first, insurance to pay for your medical expenses. As we discussed earlier, PIP is primary to all other coverages except workers' compensation. But PIP is limited. When PIP runs out, you will need to tap into the next insurance to cover those medical losses. For most people, that is their health insurance. However, some drivers—I'm one of them—carry an optional extra policy to pay for medical expenses. It's called medical payments coverage (MedPay), and it is extra insurance on the auto policy. MedPay handles the medical bills and expenses after your PIP insurance runs out and also covers any deductible on the PIP insurance coverage. In some states, MedPay is mandatory. In most, it's optional. The next tier of protection is your health insurance. Health insurance will pay your bills after workers' comp, PIP, and MedPay are exhausted. The final tier is any government insurance, such as Medicare or Medicaid.

You are legally required to use workers' comp if your accident occurred while you were working. The problem with workers' comp is that it creates a real drag on your personal injury case. The workers' comp doctors are paid by the workers' comp carrier, and they will undermine your situation more than any other type of doctor because their goal is to minimize the injury and get you back to work as fast as possible. They know what to say and do to keep the claim as low as possible.

When you're injured in a workers' comp case, your employer has the right to send you to the doctor or medical clinic with whom they have a contract. Your employer hires them to evaluate their injured workers. These doctors understand that the quicker they can get someone back on the job, the happier the employer will be, and the more likely the doctor is to continue getting these referrals. As a result, they consistently send people back to work even when the employee has lost an arm or has a major herniated disk in their neck or some other bad injury. The comp doctor is never sympathetic to your case, and they can hurt your future private injury claim against the at-fault driver.

This is not to say that workers' comp isn't a great benefit. It can be amazing if you're catastrophically injured in an accident, and the at-fault driver has little insurance, and the injury victim also has a small amount of insurance. If the other driver's insurance is not significant and you need back surgery, you're grateful for workers' comp because it'll pay 100 percent of the operation and the rehab.

However, if the insurance coverage in the case is solid—if the PIP is good, the other driver's BIL is good, or your uninsured motorist coverage is good—then your best choice is to start with workers' comp and move through it quickly. Get them to pay for the initial office visits and treatment and move to your personal injury case. You will always make out better in a personal injury case than you will in a workers' comp case because comp doesn't give you anything for pain and suffering. It only pays your medical bills and lost wages.

If you're in this situation, one way to deal with it is to go to your workers' comp carrier and ask them to settle your case early, pay you up front, and waive their right to get any money back from a future personal injury case.

For example, the comp carrier might ask how much you think your case is worth. If you need $30,000 or $40,000 for the surgery, $5,000 for physical therapy, and $1,000 for medication, you can tell the carrier that you think your case is worth $46,000 but that you're willing to accept $25,000 and will write off your right to surgery in the future. They are likely to accept an offer like that, and now you're free to start billing your PIP insurance and telling the at-fault driver's company that you'll be making a claim against his BIL coverage. Now you can go to whatever doctor you want and have that doctor say what kind of treatment you need.

This is obviously complex, so the only time we suggest you try this is when you are not really badly hurt. If you have an injury that demands significant medical intervention or coordination, get professional legal help to maximize the value of these insurances. When the damages require you to coordinate the workers' compensation coverage, the automobile insurance coverage, the health insurance, and possibly other benefits—such as long-term care, disability income, Social Security Disability (SSD), or Supplemental Security Income (SSI)—get an attorney. The best firms offer all these coordinated services on a contingency basis. Take advantage of that and get your total package of benefits maximized.

WHEN AN INSURER EXHIBITS BAD FAITH

Insurance companies have a legal obligation to protect their customers from being sued and having to pay judgments. You buy insurance because you don't want to be in a lawsuit, and you want to avoid it. But sometimes insurance companies negotiate in a way that ultimately hurts their client, and in some instances, you can turn around and sue them for bad faith.

Here's what that scenario might look like. Say you cause an accident that leaves another driver badly injured. Your insurance company is obligated to ensure you are protected from a lawsuit. If you get sued, they have to hire an attorney and pay for your defense.

But in this scenario, when the injured driver files a claim, your insurance company basically tells the driver to go to hell. Although the injured driver's medical bills are quite high, your insurance company declines the plaintiff's request that it tender your $100,000 BIL policy limit. They offer a much smaller settlement.

In response, the plaintiff hires a bulldog attorney who also demands the policy limit and lays out the extensive reasoning for that settlement. Tender the policy limits, and we can end this, the bulldog says. But your insurance company turns him down as well, even though a reasonable decision would be to tender the policy limits and settle the case.

Instead, the case drags on for two years of discovery and court hearings until the insurance company caves in and offers to tender the policy limit of $100,000. Now it's the bulldog lawyer's turn to play hardball. He tells the insurance company that he doesn't want the $100,000. He wants more—a lot more—and indicates he will take his chances with the jury.

The bulldog lawyer sues for $1 million and wins. The insurance company is on the hook for only the $100,000, but you—the client whom they promised to protect—are looking at a $900,000 judgment. You don't have that kind of money. Your only choice is to declare bankruptcy.

Or better—you can sue your own insurance company for failing to protect you when they could have settled, and should have settled, and would have settled if they had properly evaluated the case against you on a timely basis.

And that's what happens. After the case is over, you find out that the bulldog lawyer tried and tried to settle the case for

$100,000 and that your insurance company could have and should have settled. But they didn't. The bulldog now invites you to join his cause. He advises you that you can bring a "bad faith lawsuit" against your own insurance company, and you can collect the $900,000 you owe the plaintiff, which will settle the case against you and keep you out of bankruptcy.

There are two types of bad faith cases. Third-party bad faith is when your insurance company is defending you against someone else who isn't related to your insurance company policy. First-party bad faith is when you bring a legitimate insurance claim to your own company, and they tell you to go jump in a lake. An example would be if you get badly hurt by an uninsured motorist and your insurance company refuses to offer you adequate funds from your own under-insured motorist coverage.

In Florida, before you can sue an insurance company for first-party bad faith, you must give them an opportunity to settle the case. Florida has a special document called a civil remedy notice (CRN). A CRN is a Florida state-mandated document that details why you think your insurance company is behaving badly. You must file the CRN and give some details on why your carrier is wrong before you can hold them in bad faith. A CRN gives the insurance company an opportunity to correct their actions. They usually don't correct anything, but you still must jump through this hoop.

Bad faith lawsuits don't happen often, but it's not unusual for insurance companies to hurt themselves by dragging their feet in cases like the one I described above. A good example is a case I described in chapter 2 involving a motorcycle rider who had $1 million in medical bills after he was hit by another driver who carried a $100,000 BIL insurance. We contacted the at-fault driver's insurance, told them it was a big case, and offered to provide them with whatever information they needed. But all we got was radio silence.

Four months later, we sued. They had a legal obligation to investigate this case and they didn't do it. We went to mediation, and the insurers offered $500,000, but as I said, my client already had $1 million in medical bills, so we didn't accept it. If we go to trial, I will ask for more than seven figures for my client.

WHEN CAN YOU SUE?

The concept of a no-fault state has nothing to do with whether you can sue a guy who hit you. A no-fault policy just means that your insurance company doesn't consider fault when determining how much to pay you. Health insurance is a good example. If you injure your toe through your own negligence—for instance, you drop a heavy tool on your toe and break it—your health insurance company doesn't refuse to pay you because the accident was your fault. The insurance company doesn't care whose fault it is. You're the policyholder, you need medical care for your toe, and so the company is going to pay you what you have coming according to the policy you carry with them. That's what no fault is.

Workers' compensation insurance is the same way. If you trip over your own two feet at work and break your knee cap, workers' comp pays for your treatment. It doesn't matter that you are clumsy and hurt yourself. You got hurt on the job.

In the realm of auto accidents, no-fault insurance stems from some states trying to unburden the court system from small cases by forcing people to get insurance and cover themselves so they wouldn't have any significant outstanding medical bills or lost wages in small accidents. The scheme they came up with was this concept of "no fault" automobile insurance, which is the PIP (personal injury protection) coverage we've talked about. No matter who is at fault, your PIP will pay for your medical bills and sometimes even lost wages up to the coverage limits, regardless of who is at fault for causing the accident. The idea here is that if PIP covers the accident-related medical bills that are small, nobody will need to sue.

In most no-fault states, a plaintiff can't sue for future pain and suffering in these smaller, less severe cases that fall under no-fault insurance, such as PIP. In most accidents, economic damages are clear and easy to figure out. In no-fault states, you have to reach a monetary threshold for economic damages before you can sue for future pain and suffering. In other PIP states, there is a "verbal threshold," which means that a medical professional must put into the medical records written proof that the injury is "permanent within a reasonable degree of medical probability" or has "significant scarring or disfigurement," or includes a "significant loss of an important body function," or "death." The "verbal threshold" uses the medical reports to separate out the really bad permanent injuries from the temporary soft tissue injuries. The reasoning is that in small cases, there won't be any future damages. You'll heal. There's no permanent damage that's going to cause you to need future pain and suffering compensation.

Five or six of the nation's twelve no-fault states have set these monetary thresholds. The concept is that you can't sue for pain and suffering unless you have at least $2,000 in medical bills. Once you reach that threshold, the reasoning goes, that's evidence that you have had a significant amount of treatment and are likely going to need future treatment. The actual threshold comes in a variety of flavors—$2,500 or $5,000, for instance.

The other states think that's a crazy approach. They point out that one minute of treatment in the hospital will allow you to meet the threshold. You could be driven by ambulance to the hospital only to receive a Band-Aid and told to go home, and you've reached the threshold. These states say you should have a much more significant hurdle to clear before you're allowed to sue, and that hurdle should include a doctor's interpretation of your injury.

This is where the verbal threshold came from. Only a medical professional can look at an injury and say, "I believe this injury is permanent and will not go away, and I believe I'll be right more than 50 percent of the time." That is the reasonable degree of medical probability.

If you don't meet the threshold, you can still sue for your past medical bills related to the accident that are not covered by PIP or workers' comp. But the moment you do that, you may have to stop getting treatment for your injuries because those are now future bills that are not recoverable because you don't have a permanent injury within a reasonable degree of medical probability.

To complicate things further, some states' workers' compensation laws include guidelines for doctors to use when asked to determine if someone has a permanent injury or not. It tells the doctors what it takes to determine that an injury is permanent within a reasonable degree of medical probability. The American Medical Association has put out a book called the *AMA Guide to Permanent Impairment*. It gives specific findings a doctor must make to prove the injury is permanent. Doctors who understand these guidelines can quickly determine just how permanent any injury will be based on the treatment notes and an examination of the patient. Before you try and settle your case, you will need to figure out if your treatment doctor will give you a permanent impairment rating. The higher the rating, the more valuable your claim. You will want to know this before approaching any insurance company about a settlement.

These factors will all affect how you deal with insurance companies, whether they represent you or they represent the other driver. But weighing these factors is just the beginning. Having good insurance is the first step in protecting yourself from an accident. But as we'll learn in the next chapter, not all injuries suffered in an accident are physical. Some are psychological, and those types of injuries can be especially challenging to fully value.

CHAPTER THREE

DIFFERENT TYPES OF ACCIDENTS AND INJURIES

Not all motor vehicle accidents are the same. The accidents involving motorcycles, boats, commercial vehicles, and trains, for instance, are usually vastly different than automobile accidents.

In truth, every accident has a unique set of circumstances, and each circumstance will affect your injuries, how you file your claim, and whether you hire an attorney to help you. This chapter explores some of the unusual circumstances you may encounter and how to best respond to them.

I'll start with the story of Joe Nye, who was a truck driver whose route took him along the eastern seaboard of Florida. One day, he was returning home after dropping off a load. He was bobtailing, which means he was driving the truck portion of his rig and wasn't hauling a box trailer. The fog was dense as he moved south on Florida's turnpike north of Palm Beach. All of a sudden, a passenger vehicle passed him at high speed, and Joe watched in horror as that driver lost control of their vehicle and collided with another car right in Joe's path.

Joe had no choice and was forced to steer off the highway and into the roadside canal running parallel to the turnpike. This was not a drainage ditch or a shallow diversion channel. This was a deep, substantial waterway that was home to alligators, fish, snakes, and who knows what else. His truck hurtled into the water and started sinking. As the water rose around him, Joe forced his way out of the truck. He had to swim a short distance to get to the shoreline of the canal. Not far away, an alligator slithered off the swale and into the water. Not all alligators are frightened of people, but fortunately, this one was.

Joe reached solid ground and quickly made his way back up to the highway. He spotted the two cars in the accident. One was on its side. He ran over to it. As he got closer, he could see the car that had sped by him on its side. Inside, the driver, his wife, and their small child were trapped in the wreckage. The child was in his mother's arms, half in and half out of the twisted metal, but the mother couldn't get the child out. Joe ran over to help, but he could not remove the child. The ambulance hadn't arrived yet, and Joe was forced to watch as this child died right in front of him. To this day, that child haunts Joe in his sleep.

I tell Joe's story because it illustrates how some motor vehicle accidents inflict deeper wounds than others. Joe lost his truck and had to swim to safety in alligator-infested waters, but he walked away from the accident and did not suffer debilitating physical injuries. Physically, he would be fine.

But the emotional trauma of watching that child die was not so easy for Joe to recover from. He developed posttraumatic stress. He was deeply depressed, and his overall enjoyment in life was diminished. He could not get the image of this dying child out of his head. He couldn't work, and he didn't even want to drive his truck anymore. It was going to take therapy, time, and effort on Joe's part to heal the psychic wounds he suffered when that driver sped past him in the fog and caused this crash.

In cases like this, it's imperative that someone like Joe get a lawyer to represent him. All of the things that Joe endured—the loss of his truck, the loss of work time, and the psychological scarring—must be entered into the ledger of what Joe Nye is owed because of this accident.

But it's extremely difficult for a victim—someone like Joe—to make a case for their emotional trauma to an insurance adjuster. An adjuster just won't buy it. They'll see it as self-serving, overstated, or untrue.

So Joe did the right thing and hired us to represent him. We got him the medical help he needed to feel better and documented his injury. We were able to show how this injury was real, and that proof would have allowed a jury to understand the real nature and extent of the injury and feel for Joe. That got him the compensation he deserved.

BAD BEHAVIOR BY THE DEFENDANT

Another factor, in any case, is bad behavior on the part of the defendant. Not only do defendants behave badly when they cause an accident, but some defendants behave badly afterward. They get aggressive. They refuse to apologize. They try to intimidate the plaintiff into taking some or all of the responsibility. When that happens, it also drives value into a case and makes it worth more.

I first noticed this in medical malpractice cases. The case might be worth only $100,000, but when the doctor was arrogant, rude, or insensitive before or after the incident, a jury will punish that behavior by awarding the plaintiff millions of dollars. When you're a plaintiff's lawyer, you have to create a hero (your client, the plaintiff) and a villain (the defendant who caused the accident). When the defendant behaves badly, it's much easier to make them a villain. In one instance, we drove so much emotion into the case that the jury didn't give us what we wanted—they gave twice what we asked for! That case taught us how jurors relate to injustice, fraud, and dishonesty.

In another case, my client was horribly injured when he was struck by a car driven by a young woman who was out with her two sisters. My client was left blinded and paralyzed. He had over a million dollars in medical bills. He would be in a wheelchair for the rest of his life. At trial, we asked for $30 million.

The defense lawyer put up little or no fight during the trial. He rarely cross-examined anyone, and when he did, he apologized left and right for the damage caused by this accident. He was respectful and empathetic. He basically fell on his sword, which made it difficult to paint him or his client as a villain before the jury.

But then, in his closing, he pleaded with the jury for a "reasonable" settlement. He thought $3 million or $4 million was the proper settlement. I was worried. The jury could easily have been persuaded to award only $3 million. The case was tragic, but the economic damages were only $1 million, so $3 million sounded reasonable. Our request for a range of $15 million to $30 million was too much for the case. Then the defendant's attorney erred. He said my client's suffering didn't warrant allowing a "lottery win."

You're not allowed to say that in court, but I didn't object. I was happy. I wanted to respond to the statement, and I jumped on it in my rebuttal closing argument. "No one who has been blinded and has to sit in a wheelchair for the rest of their life can be considered a lottery winner," I said. "To say so is cruel and callous."

I addressed the jury: "How much money would make it worthwhile for you to be paralyzed and blind for the rest of your life? Ladies and gentlemen, even $30 million are not enough to serve justice in this case, but this is the award you should return to my client."

In the end, the jury awarded us between $8 million and $9 million. It was less than what we hoped but triple what the defense attorney asked for. And it proved an important point: good behavior counts, too.

The key is to document the behavior. Document the rage. Document the dishonesty. Every time you can create a good-guy-versus-bad-guy scenario, you must preserve that moment.

SEVERITY OF INJURY

One thing I've learned over the years is that it's very difficult for adjusters to account for emotional injuries. They just won't do it.

Another thing to keep in mind if you are pursuing your own case is that adjusters get nervous when the numbers get big. They will not give you fair values in cases like that. For example, I was advising another attorney—her name was Irene—who had a client injured in an accident caused by someone else. The other driver had an insurance policy with a $1 million limit on it, and our client had over $200,000 in medical bills. In my mind, this was a case worth $500,000 or $550,000. So we asked for $1 million.

The adjuster's initial offer was $134,000.

When an adjuster starts out that far away from what the case is truly worth, you often have no choice but to sue. When the adjuster starts out at $134,000 in what should be a half-million-dollar case, you might be able to drag him to $200,000 and then possibly $225,000. But that's as far as he'll usually go. If you entertain an offer like that, you'll spend the next six months negotiating and never get the number up to where it should be.

When you receive a low-ball offer, decide quickly whether to take it. Sometimes, life events warrant taking a quick offer. Perhaps you are moving or leaving to join the circus. (Yes, this really happened to me in a case. The week before trial, my client announced that she had fallen in love with Ed the elephant trainer at Ringling Bros. Circus and was leaving that Sunday. She would not be able to go to trial with me. Not a fake story!)

You may be an excellent negotiator, know how to write a great demand letter, be able to drive value into your case, and still get an insultingly low offer from the claims adjuster. Your only recourse in situations like that is to reject the low-ball offer, hire an attorney, and file a lawsuit. If you're determined to handle a severe-injury case yourself, be prepared to take a little or even a lot less than you would get with an attorney. The only time it can benefit the plaintiff to represent themselves is when the value of the case is below $100,000, or the plaintiff has a compelling reason to undersell the case and take a lot less.

In Joe Nye's case, he settled his case after the canal accident for close to $1 million. When you watch a child die, the image is burned into your brain, and the sadness gets a grip on your sensibilities. A grim melancholy settles over you, and you find you have to spend years in therapy to overcome that. But to get fair compensation for that pain, you've got to complain about it, and you have to get treatment for it. It's got to be real, and the other side has to believe you by seeing it in your medical records. And again, you need a third party to make this argument for you. You need a lawyer.

SEVERITY OF ACCIDENTS

Certain types of accidents create circumstances that make it difficult for plaintiffs to negotiate themselves.

Motorcycle accidents often fall into this category. Motorcycles have no protective cage to help riders survive a crash. Motorcycles also tend to go from standstill to high rates of velocity and then from a high rate of speed to a standstill very rapidly. That's a bad combination. Motorcycle accidents tend to be the most dangerous types of accidents we see.

Another key reason for this is that most automobile drivers simply do not see motorcycles. It's not because the motorcycles are not there. It's because drivers have been trained to look out for other cars and trucks. You might hear a motorcycle, and you might be looking right at it, but your mind often does not perceive it. Most motorcycle accidents occur not because the motorcyclist was negligent but because the driver of the car that pulled out in front of them wasn't aware they were there.

We've had hundreds of motorcycle-involved cases in our office, and when we interview the defendants, the most common thing we hear is, "The motorcycle must have been moving at incredibly high speeds because when I looked, he wasn't there and then suddenly he was." It's true that motorcycles are engineered to go from zero to sixty in a matter of seconds, but I can tell you we've had far too many cases where the motorcyclist tells us that they made eye contact with the driver, that they were traveling at a safe speed, and still the defendant car driver pulled out right in front of them. The result is a 300- or 400-pound motorcycle being struck by a 3,000-pound car.

On top of that, many motorcyclists aren't wearing proper safety equipment. Some states, like Florida, still do not make motorcycle helmets mandatory. You have motorcyclists tooling around in the warm air with no head protection. They tell themselves to slow down, drive safely, stay in the slow lane. But even at 45 miles per hour in the slow lane, automobiles still find ways to hit them.

It's a false stereotype to suggest that motorcycle riders are reckless. We have an attorney in our office who was a motorcycle police officer for twenty years. He has seen thousands of accidents and was a professional accident investigator. He will tell you how most motorcycle accident cases involve a responsible motorcyclist and an automobile driver who simply did not see the motorcycle. That is not to say that the young riders on racing motorcycles—those Suzuki sportbikes are an example—are not often recklessly speeding down the highway on their crotch rockets. These bikes are lightweight and have forward-leaning ergonomics that encourage riders to carve corners and fly down straightaways. Accidents involving those bikes are never pretty.

My wife and daughter were driving down the highway not long ago when they were passed by one of these bikes traveling at over 100 miles an hour. A mile later, at a bend in the highway, they came upon the awful accident site. The rider lost control in the turn and struck a concrete barrier. People were already rushing to where he was sprawled out on the shoulder. My daughter came home and said, "Daddy, promise me you will never get a motorcycle."

The larger motorcycles—called cruisers or touring bikes—are usually ridden in a much safer fashion. This is particularly true when the riders are following each other in a group. Drivers may not easily see a single rider, but they will see groups of riders, and they certainly will hear that group as they approach.

Despite the dangers, a lot of motorcycle accidents are minor enough and the insurance coverage so low that riders can represent themselves if they are victims of an accident. And even though insurance companies like to throw shade on the injuries you claim in an auto accident—they'll argue that your sore neck was caused by playing football years ago, for instance—the injuries suffered in a motorcycle accident are usually pretty apparent. That makes these cases easier for the plaintiff to handle on their own. More often than not, the motorcycle rider is not at fault, and the injury is easy to see and believable. The insurance is almost always on the defendant. Getting to a fair number for minor injuries is a pretty easy negotiation.

This is not often the case with riders on crotch rockets. If you're a teenage kid on a crotch rocket, you're probably out there speeding around, leaning into corners, and generally acting like a jerk. They usually end up getting hurt so badly that it's ridiculous. And it's their fault. This makes it difficult for them to collect, even when they are not riding like a jerk. There is a huge prejudice against these riders based on a community belief about how they are ridden. But if the other driver was even partially responsible, a motorcyclist can still collect the automobile driver's portion of the blame. To get there, however, motorcycle riders often must overcome the inherent prejudice against them. This is a combination where an attorney specializing in motorcycle injuries can help. These attorneys will be sympathetic and understand the rules and details of motorcycle accidents. The insurance adjuster is not immune to prejudice against motorcycle riders. They don't always appreciate the danger a significant motorcycle accident holds against their client. That can lead to bad decision making by the adjuster, and that can lead to a good situation for the injured victim if they hire a smart lawyer.

GOOD FAITH, BAD FAITH

Let me explain how that prejudice sometimes shows up.

I'm involved in a case where I represent a motorcycle rider who was badly injured when a vehicle pulled out from a side street and slammed into my client. My client was in the hospital for thirty days.

The accident occurred when he was riding down one of our main north-south surface roads. It's a big thoroughfare, with three lanes of traffic in each direction, and my client was heading north in the slow lane. No one else was on the road.

The other driver came in from the east and stopped at a stop sign for a left-hand turn. She planned to cross the three lanes of northbound traffic before curling south and heading down the road in the opposite direction. She gunned the engine at the precise moment that my client was passing in front of her, slamming sidelong into him. Someone watching from above would swear that she was waiting for just the right moment to hit him like she'd been taking aim or something. My client was badly injured. The woman carried $100,000 in bodily injury liability.

We contacted the woman's insurance company and explained that our client was facing hundreds of thousands of dollars in medical bills. After thirty days in the hospital, you can imagine how large his medical bills were.

A smart adjuster would have immediately tendered the woman's policy limits and released the full $100,000. That's all they were obligated to pay, and they could have met their obligation by cutting a check for the coverage the woman carried. This would have protected them and their client from being sued.

But because our client was a motorcyclist, the insurance seemed to think he somehow shared some of the responsibility for the accident. They assumed because he rode a motorcycle that he was reckless or negligent in some way. As a result, they didn't do anything. They didn't respond to our letter. They didn't try to evaluate the case. They didn't try to settle. They said nothing. They didn't even contact their client to ask her about the accident.

After ninety days, we filed a lawsuit. At her deposition, the automobile driver broke down in tears. She admitted that she plowed into our client, and she said she didn't think our client had been speeding. She hadn't seen him until she was running into him. She felt terrible, she said. "I think about it every night. I feel guilty. I feel terrible for him. I want to do whatever I can to make it right."

This illustrates how insurance companies sometimes don't bargain in good faith. Florida is one of the states that have laws about this behavior. If an insurance company acts in bad faith and their client is sued as a result—precisely what happened in this case—then the insurance company can be held responsible.

The insurance company could have gotten out of this mess by paying our client the $100,000 the woman had in her policy. We ended up getting our client $1.75 million.

BOATING ACCIDENTS

Boating accidents are another type of vehicular mishap that you'll typically need a lawyer to sort out. Boats are governed by a whole different set of rules, and those rules aren't normally what people would become familiar with through everyday life. There are the federal maritime laws, international maritime laws three miles out to sea, the cruise industry contractual rules, international treaties that control injuries to workers and guests, the Death on the High Seas Act, the Defense Base Act, the Jones Act, and many more laws affecting travel on the high seas.

Many people don't realize that the owner, or captain, of a boat is fully responsible for the safety of all passengers. So if you're piloting your boat and you hit a wave that knocks someone to the floor of your vessel, it's the captain's fault, not the passenger's. What's more, very little safety equipment is required on a boat. There are no seat belts or straps, and the cushions move. To get insurance on your boat, the only safety equipment you need is a flotation device, a fire extinguisher, a whistle, and a flare.

Recreation boats are made from hard, Kevlar, fiberglass, steel, or wood shells, so when you go up and down, fall, or trip in this rocking, slippery, wet, hard surface, you are apt to get hurt. Those who are swimming, diving, or waterskiing off the boat are also in danger from other boats. You are in more danger from other boats than from anything that lives in the sea. You should be more afraid of another boat than about a shark swimming beside you.

We typically see two types of boating cases more than others: accidents that occur on a cruise ship and accidents involving two or more private vessels. Occasionally, we have a boat hitting a swimmer with terrible consequences. These incidents all have their own set of rules, most of which are different from the rules governing other motor vehicles. Fortunately, one of our lawyers is a specialist in cruise and boat accidents. He concentrated on maritime law in law school and moved to Florida from Ohio just to be near the sea and practice maritime law.

CRUISE SHIPS

If you're injured on a cruise ship, your case has to be handled according to the following rules:

- You must notify the cruise line within six months of your injury. This is easy because most people injured on a cruise will visit the doctor on the ship and file an incident report.
- You must file a lawsuit within a year of your accident.
- You have to sue within the cruise line's jurisdiction. Most of the cruise lines operate out of Miami, although a few operate out of Seattle. What this means is that you have to hire an attorney who has been admitted to practice law in the Southern District of Florida.

You rarely can settle a cruise ship lawsuit in less than a year. Cruise lines usually settle all their own cases and don't use insurance companies. Most offers they make before then are low-ball bullshit offers, so you almost always have to sue to get fair compensation. Don't wait on a cruise accident case. For almost all cruise lines, call an attorney in South Florida. If you are hurt on a Holland America cruise, call someone in Seattle. We get cruise accident calls for all cruise lines; you are welcome to call our office for a free referral as well. The maritime industry is small, and we can help you find the exact right lawyer for your case.

PRIVATE BOAT ACCIDENTS

With recreational boaters, the conflicts usually involve collisions or similar mishaps. We rarely see cases where the captain of a commercial vessel or small ship is sued by injured passengers. Usually, we get calls when weekend warrior boaters have messed up. These nonprofessional boaters hit each other, they hit piers, they hit buoy markers, and they hit pylons. Most boaters are not out on the water as much as they are on the road, and boats are often more challenging to navigate than cars. First of all, you think you aren't moving fast because the water is so big and open and expansive. But then when you approach an obstacle, it suddenly feels like it's right on top of you, and you have no easy way to slow down or stop.

What's more, most boat owners get very little training. Most learn by trial and error. We make automobile drivers take driver's education and a state-required driving test before we allow them out on the road. But anyone who wants to captain a boat only needs to buy a boat, launch it, and start ripping through the Intracoastal Waterway with a bunch of people on board.

There are a lot of regulations on how to sail a boat and navigate public waterways, but no one reads them or knows them. For instance, when you launch your boat, you're supposed to beep your horn twice to let everyone else know you're leaving the pier. No one does this.

We had one client who was approaching a public dock. Another guy was launching his boat. So my client stopped advancing and just floated in place while he waited for that slip position to open up by the pier. Our client left the captain's chair for a few moments to get something from the bulkhead, and suddenly, the other boat, without sounding his horn, roared away from the pier and crashed into my client's boat, pitching him to the deck and breaking his leg badly.

During depositions, the other boater claimed my client was negligent and should not have left his position at the helm, even though he was floating in a still position. The other boater claimed to be a "professional captain." He insisted at his deposition that maritime law required my client to not leave the steering wheel. He also said that my client had to make way for anyone departing the dock.

"Really?" I said. "Where is that in the regulations? I brought the code with me."

Of course, he couldn't do that because that regulation doesn't exist. But since this "professional captain" was so up on the rules, I asked him if he'd sounded his horn before pulling away.

"My horn? No. Why should I?"

I guess he wasn't as familiar with the rule that requires he blow his horn twice to warn others to make way. He was at fault for causing the accident, but he didn't realize it because he didn't know the rules. Finding fault in boating is like finding fault in anything: the way to determine who is right and who is wrong is by knowing the rules and applying the rules. Most people don't know the rules on the water, so those who take the time to learn them have a distinct advantage. After depositions, the captain's insurance company tendered the policy limits for my client, and we didn't have to try the case.

What complicates things—at least here in Florida—is that boat owners are not required to carry insurance. That doesn't mean you can't get insurance. I have insurance on my boat, and I think everyone should carry insurance if they own a boat. It's crazy not to. If you have one bad accident, you can be looking at bankruptcy.

The most common boating accidents we see are when a captain drives recklessly and injures a passenger. The passenger gets knocked to the deck and breaks something or cracks their head on a thwart or something. Sometimes a passenger gets knocked into the water, and the captain backs over them with his propeller. That's a particularly gruesome accident. We also see situations where a boat captain comes into a dock too fast, and one of the passengers sticks out a leg to try to stop the boat from hitting the dock. They don't realize how much force the boat has, or else they get their leg trapped between the dock and the boat. That's pretty common.

The second most common accident is when boaters slam into other boats.

Jet skis are another common source of accidents. People don't realize that the only way a jet ski will turn is if it's under power. People will be headed toward an immovable object like a channel pylon or a dock, and they release the throttle. But when they try to turn, the jet ski just keeps going, and they crash.

LEARN THE RULES FOR YOUR STATE

Accidents involving cars and trains are very rare, and my office has little experience with them. I know enough about them to say that if you have a case like that, don't just get an attorney. Get an attorney who tries those cases all the time.

I had a colleague who represented a client who was injured by a train. The crossing guard mechanism had failed, and my friend's client drove right in front of an oncoming train, which clipped his car in the rear. The railroad was clearly at fault, and there was even a video of the accident. It was open and shut. But it wasn't until my friend consulted with an expert that he was able to get any decent money out of the railroad. He needed help from someone familiar with the multitude of federal regulations concerning railroads.

And in many ways, this is what individual motorists must

do if they want to represent themselves in a motor vehicle accident—they have to know the rules in their states. Usually, it's just a matter of Googling insurance requirements for your own state. It's important to do this before you meet with an insurance agent to set your policy. The agent could recommend coverage that's twice what the state requires, and when that happens, you need to be aware of it and ask the agent to explain their recommendation.

THE WORST THING YOU CAN DO

Regardless of what state you live in, the worst thing you can do as a driver is to exhibit bad behavior behind the wheel. Bad behavior includes using any substance that will cause your driving to be impaired, be it alcohol, drugs, marijuana, or anything like that. That's a mistake on a colossal scale. Impairment drives all damages in the case and will drive punitive damages as well. And even though you can get out from under some damages by filing for bankruptcy protection, bankruptcy won't help you get out from under a big punitive damage award against you. You can't get rid of it.

The second-worst thing you can do is be reckless in how you interact with technology while driving, particularly handheld technology. If you're caught working on your handheld technology in the car at the time of an accident, authorities will treat it the same as if you were drinking. You will get punished in a way that is punitive. And again, those punitive damages can't be discharged through bankruptcy.

Add these distractions to the fact that most people routinely drive on rural, two-lane roads where the margin for error is minimal. There are no shoulders, no center divider, and little traffic enforcement. It's a recipe for head-on collisions, which are the worst kind of accident you can have. I think self-driving technology that warns you when you drift will help and eventually will be standard in all cars, but we're still far away from that being ubiquitous technology.

Highways, because of the high speed and number of cars, can be dangerous, but most accidents occur at intersections. All sorts of unfortunate things happen at intersections. Drivers blow through red lights or ignore stop signs. People turn in front of oncoming cars and arrive at the intersection too fast and rear-end a waiting vehicle. People don't pay attention to crosswalks and plow into pedestrians. Intersections are confusing and dangerous.

That's why you see so many towns around the country replacing them with roundabouts. Some drivers are baffled by roundabouts, but the truth is, they are more efficient and safer than regular intersections. Washington, DC, is filled with them, and sometimes five, six, or seven different streets feed into a roundabout. You'd think there would be an accident every couple of minutes, but there is seldom an accident. Meanwhile, at a traditional intersection two miles away, people are hitting each other left and right. State officials in Washington did a study in 2018 that showed roundabouts are between 75 percent and 90 percent safer than traditional four-way intersections.

Cars have become safer over the years by adding seat belts, airbags, tempered glass, unbreakable seatbacks, headrests so we don't snap our necks, roll bars, and shoulder straps. And manufacturers are always looking for new safety improvements. For instance, I think self-driving cars will improve highway safety. I have an assisted-driving car that will hold its lane and maintain its speed, stop at all lights and stop signs, and continually remind you to stay alert and engaged in the driving process. It will slow down for people in front of me and will react if another vehicle changing lanes starts to pull into me.

With all these safety improvements, you have to wonder why deaths from car accidents remain so high. According to the National Highway Traffic Safety Administration, the number of people killed in motor vehicle accidents declined after 2008 but has been steadily growing each year since. Why can't we bring that number down?

Because no matter how safe we make cars, we still find ways to injure or kill ourselves in cars.

If you're one of the more than two million people injured each year in a motor vehicle accident, you need to be aware of what your rights are and how to make yourself whole again. In our next chapter, we'll explore the types of injuries people face and how they should approach their treatment.

CHAPTER FOUR

UNDERSTANDING MEDICAL TREATMENT

We recently represented a woman who had been badly injured in an auto accident that wasn't her fault. She had a stack of medical bills for her treatments, and she also had evidence that she would need future surgery and other medical procedures. What's more, she'd lost a lot of time away from work, and that had also hurt financially. This accident had a devastating impact on her life. Clearly, she had endured a lot of pain and suffering.

We could not reach a settlement agreement with the insurance company, so the case went to trial. The jury awarded our client $120,000 for her past medical bills and $150,000 for future surgeries. They also gave her $100,000 for past and future lost wages. So the total the jury awarded her for her documented economic damages amounted to $280,000.

How much do you think they gave her for pain and suffering?

If you answered $280,000, $560,000, or $840,000, you would be in the same ballpark we believed the jury should award. Our client had been through hell, so we asked them for three times her economic damages. Normal and reasonable. We felt just normal pain and suffering in a case like this was worth at least as much as her economic damages, but we felt she had experienced a higher level of these non-economic damages and deserved to be compensated for it by the company representing the driver who caused that pain and suffering.

So we were expecting a total verdict of somewhere between $500,000 and $700,000.

We got much less. The jury awarded our client $2,000 for past pain and suffering and $5,000 for future pain and suffering. Seven thousand dollars for total for pain and suffering! Incredible and callous. We had tried a great case. Our client testified well. The defendant had not made a huge impression. But someone on that jury fought hard against pain and suffering damages.

The point here is that you never know what a jury will decide on noneconomic damages. A trial lawyer I know decided to take a small soft-tissue-injury case to trial. He was going to ask for $85,000 total. A famous rich person somehow was put on the jury. I don't know how often rich and famous people get put on juries, but it does happen. In the jury room at the end of the case, the rich guy convinced the rest of the jurors that my buddy, the plaintiff's attorney, was an idiot who didn't know the value of the injury and argued that the plaintiff needed $1.5 million to be fully compensated. The jury awarded him $1.5 million. My point is that pain and suffering are hard to determine, and like art, the value of a case is in the eyes of the beholder.

Medical bills, property damage, lost wages—all the economic damages—are straightforward and easy to calculate. The emotional or psychic damage caused by a tragic accident is much more difficult to put a number on. In my case, there may have been someone on the jury who didn't believe people should be compensated for pain and suffering. Or maybe they didn't like something my client said in her testimony. There could have been any one of a gazillion reasons why they came back with that terribly low pain and suffering verdict. By the same token, the leader of my buddy's jury felt otherwise about pain and suffering and saw it as something that had real consequences—even more than my friend believed could be explained to the jury.

You just don't know what the jury will do. Regardless of the circumstances in your case, you always run the risk of getting very little for your pain and suffering.

Adjusters know this. That's why adjusters don't give much, if anything, for noneconomic damages. Adjusters will discount your pain and suffering to zero.

If you are considering handling your own case instead of hiring a lawyer, you have to recognize that the best way to succeed is to make your economic damages as big as they can be because you can't bank on getting much for noneconomic damages. You can't count on getting a fair shake on pain and suffering. You can certainly make it part of your demand, but it will be discounted. If you want your case settled without litigation, you're going to have to accept this fact. If they aren't going to give it to an attorney—as in the case I just described—they certainly aren't going to give it to you. That is okay if your expectations are in line and if you have good evidence of past and future economic loss, lost wages, and medical damages.

GETTING MEDICAL TREATMENT

If you've been injured in an auto accident, it's crucial that you get in to see your doctor as soon as possible. Although some injuries may not have been manifested yet in physical pain and you're not fully aware of them, if you don't seek medical treatment immediately after an accident, you give the insurance company an opportunity to claim that your injuries didn't occur during the accident but after the accident.

I had one client, Vincent, who was injured in a major car accident. He went to the hospital and complained about his neck and his back. His wrist was also hurting him, but he assumed it was just a sprain and it would get better on its own, so he didn't mention it at the time. Just before the collision, he had been reaching into the back seat with his right hand but had thrown his arm forward to brace it against the dashboard just before the crash. His wrist took a pounding from the sudden impact.

A week later, Vince told his orthopedist that his wrist wasn't healing the way he expected it would. The doctor examined it and found that my client's scaphoid bone in his wrist was broken. That kind of break doesn't heal on its own and requires surgery to mend the broken bone with pins and screws. It is a common impact injury that doesn't cause the hand to stop working, and as such, it is easy to think of it as something that would easily heal.

So we included the surgery and rehab costs in our demand letter to the insurance company, and they challenged us on it. They noted that scaphoid injuries are uncommon in auto accidents and insisted that this injury happened sometime in the week after the accident. They didn't believe Vince and implied that we were lying, committing fraud, and just trying to make the case bigger than it was.

When this kind of thing happens, your only recourse is to sue and take the case to trial. Then it comes down to the believability of the client, and Vince was a believable guy.

Another thing to keep in mind is that hospitals and primary care physicians are not looking to find problems and diagnose them. They are merely looking to ease your pain and send you off to the right specialist. They'll say, "You've got pain here and here and strains there and elsewhere, go see your orthopedist."

These visits will not help your case because these doctors are not fully exploring what kind of injuries you've suffered. They'll tell you that you may have torn your anterior cruciate ligament or something, but they'll send you to another doctor for the MRI you need to verify that.

That doesn't mean you should skip that trip to the hospital. Those visits prove that after the accident, you had enough pain to go to the hospital and that connectivity of pain to the accident is worth the cost of your hospital visit. Plus, the hospital can rule out major injuries.

However, it's vital that you complain about every minor

ache and pain from the hair on your head to the nail on your toe and everything in between. If it hurts to urinate or defecate, that is extremely important to describe. Many times, impaired spinal injuries reveal themselves in incontinence. If it bothers you to bend over to your left or right. If your eye is twitching. Whatever it is—even if it's tiny—make sure the people treating you know and make note of it. These aches and pains may indicate an underlying problem that will come out later. Right after an accident, you've got all the adrenaline in your system, and your body hasn't fully reacted. It's not sore yet, and you're able to move. In two or three days, you're going to feel much worse.

THE INJURIES YOU DON'T SEE

Sudden, dramatic incidents—such as when a truck races through a red light and clips your front end as you're moving through an intersection—can trigger an adrenaline spike that camouflages your pain and the full extent of your injuries. You may walk away from the wreckage with minor aches, only to have bruising and waves of nausea, dizziness, and pain strike hours later.

What's more, you may have any one of a number of "invisible injuries" that are not immediately apparent to you or someone treating you. For example, you might have:

Organ damage. Internal injuries are often the most difficult injuries to overcome. Their effect can be traumatic. In many head-on collisions, the driver's body is slammed against the steering wheel. This can fracture a rib, which can puncture a lung, but the only visible sign is some bruising. We had one patient who survived a head-on collision and was released from the hospital on the same day as the accident. Two weeks later, he was back in the hospital—this time for five days—with a hemothorax. The pleural cavity in his chest had been slowly filling with blood for two weeks because the doctors missed some internal bleeding. Your liver and kidneys are also susceptible to injury in a car crash because neither organ is protected by bones. Kidney damage is common in traffic accidents and can leave you with intense pain, nausea, and fainting.

Traumatic brain injuries are also common in auto accidents, even relatively mild fender benders. In fact, modern medicine is realizing that undiagnosed mild traumatic brain injury (mTBI) is at epidemic levels from automobile accidents. The symptoms include nausea, vomiting, chronic headaches, forgetfulness, insomnia, and seizures. Any "fogginess," quick blackouts, or inability to remember (also called focal amnesia) is a part of an mTBI. Doctors are still learning about this injury, but we know it can occur even when the skull is not wounded. The sheer force of a car crash can cause the brain to collide against the hard bone inside the skull. The car and your head stop, but your brain continues to move until it hits the inside of your skull. There might be bruising or bleeding that are not immediately apparent. We'll talk about how to determine and document traumatic brain injuries later in this chapter when we talk about "The Tests That You Need." Any mTBI is worth a LOT of money. Never think, *I will get over it*. If your spouse or significant other tells you that your behavior, humor, demeanor, memory, or any other behavior changes after an accident seems off, you need to be checked for an mTBI.

Nerve damage. Nerve injuries are classified by levels of severity, from neurapraxia, the mildest form, to brachial plexus avulsion, when the nerve root is torn from your spine. Whiplash is a kind of nerve damage where your head whips back and forth, stretching or pinching your nerves. Even the mildest forms of nerve damage can take months to heal. Some never heal.

These are just a few of the more common hidden injuries. Others include herniated disks, compartment syndrome, torn rotator cuffs, a torn labrum in your shoulder or hips, shoulder sprains and strains, and brain damage.

SEEING THE RIGHT DOCTOR

After an injury accident, you can go see your primary care physician, but it's better to go to the hospital or an urgent care facility. There is an emotional component that gets expressed when you go to the hospital. Most people don't go to the hospital unless they're afraid. No one goes to the hospital for the fun of it. So by going to the hospital, you are establishing the fear and uncertainty you felt in the aftermath of the accident.

I don't recommend going to a primary care physician. They do not treat injuries well. If one of my clients is going to their primary care physician instead of the hospital, I like to talk to the doctor ahead of time to let them know what we are looking for from the visit.

Some people with health insurance or an HMO may think they have to go to the primary care physician first. But as we detailed in chapter 2, most states have a PIP or MedPay policy that allows you to get your initial medical care covered by something other than your health insurance policy. You need to stay away from your HMO doctor because they are trained to be as conservative as possible. Many are being paid to make sure that you don't go to expensive specialists. If you go to the hospital, the hospital can refer you to a specialist and you can skip your primary care physician.

If you're referred to a neurologist, orthopedist, chiropractor, or some other kind of specialist, do some research before choosing. Look for a doctor who has experience in auto accident cases. Look for someone who sees accident victims regularly because they understand the game, they understand how insurance companies work, and they know what needs to be put into a medical report to prove injury. They understand how to document injury in a way that an insurance company will recognize it and value it. There are doctors who specialize in that. Finding a solid and experienced injury doctor is important. This doctor will understand that they must look at their patient's physical well-being and put into their written findings all the nuanced things the patient indicates about the injury. The doctor understands what to ask to elicit the right responses that show injury. The doctor doesn't rely on the patient alone to understand their injury. As I noted before, an older woman who is slightly incontinent after an accident may think that it is due to nervousness, but the doctor will know to check to see if it is a spinal injury. Good medical notes in the initial appointments allow the doctor to look back at those notes weeks later and show how the patient expressed the beginning of an injury that now has a need for surgery to resolve the growing problem. The beginnings of that injury were caught by the smart doctor in the first couple of appointments. They can look at the patient's history and medical tests and say, "This is what happened to them, and this is what they are looking at in the future." You need someone who can holistically understand and describe how this accident hurt this human being.

A perfect example is spinal injuries. Your spine is made up of bones called vertebrae, which sit on cushions between them called intervertebral disks. The ability to move and bend so easily is because of those disks. The disk is made up of two basic parts. There is the inside jelly-like material called the nucleus pulposus, and the hard shell holding in the jelly is called the annulus fibrosus. The annulus fibrosus is like a radial tire with small cords going around it wrapping the jelly inside tightly like a hardball. The cushion allows the vertebrae to bend and move.

However, in a car accident, the head can snap forward and back so quickly that the bones of the vertebrae catch a part of the annulus and make a small cut in it called an annular tear. That in itself will cause some pain, but then over time, maybe four or five weeks, the nucleus pulposus leaks out and starts to touch the nerves of the spine. That causes tremendous pain, weakness, numbness, and associated problems. A good doctor will document the possibility of this early in an injury case. Then five weeks later, when weakness or numbness becomes present, it isn't a surprise or fake new injury. It is the well-reasoned result of an injury that occurred during the accident. Getting an MRI is necessary, and the herniated disk will then be easy to see. The future need for surgery is also well documented, and the case comes together like a perfect story. The adjuster will appreciate the well-documented medical information, and the policy will be timely tendered. The end!

But all that requires finding great medical doctors. When it comes to the documentation necessary to prove a legal case, the medical field has very weak standards. To avoid malpractice, many doctors only have to record what's necessary to show that they treated someone and that the patient had a positive outcome. Then they can release the injury victim from medical care and kill the injury case with terrible documentation.

Chiropractors, however, are different. They understand the auto insurance game and are an advocate for their patient. If you don't know where else to go for medical treatment, you usually can't go wrong starting with a chiropractor and having them get you to the right orthopedist or neurologist. Chiropractors understand that a lot of their cases will come from auto accidents and slip-and-fall cases, so they are attentive to the needs of patients who fall into that category. They will treat you and give you what you need to be able to make money and pay them for your treatment. They are sensitive to your situation and what you're going through because they see it all the time.

Here's an example: A patient who comes in for chiropractic treatment after hurting his neck in an auto accident may need additional diagnostic testing that another patient with the same injury might not need.

Say one patient comes in with a sore neck he developed while building a patio and another patient comes in with a sore neck he developed after an auto accident: same pain, same area, same level of injury. The chiropractor treats both patients identically, and after four weeks, both are still stiff but feeling better and enjoying a better range of motion.

The patio guy will probably continue to get treatment for a few more weeks before he's sent on his way to finish the patio.

The auto accident patient will need an MRI after four weeks. MRIs often don't show acute injuries—the problems picked up on an MRI often need a little time to develop—but this MRI shows a bulging disk. Now you have an objective injury that you can connect to the auto accident and include in your demand letter to the insurance company. This injury documentation is one way a chiropractor will help you. That MRI isn't going to get you different treatment. It will, however, be a photo of your injury. Yes, it's an expensive photo but worth it when you are negotiating an injury settlement.

The better chiropractors are getting training and experience with traumatic brain injury. They are becoming more aware of it, and they're documenting it when they see it. Most medical doctors don't even pay attention to traumatic brain injury. But mTBI is a common and severe injury resulting from auto accidents today. People suffering from mTBI deserve compensation for their economic and noneconomic losses that result from it.

There is also a growing cadre of orthopedists who are developing the same sensitivity to accident cases as chiropractors. Orthopedists used to live in an independent world where they could say, "I don't care where the injury occurred; just let me fix your broken arm." Many were highfalutin about it and came across as aloof. But as the world of medicine has become more competitive and doctors have lost some prestige by allowing corporations to take over their medical practices, orthopedists have looked for new avenues to regain their independence and still make a lot of money. Personal injury has become one of those avenues. They can make two or three times for a surgery in a personal injury case than they would through a private insurance case. So all of a sudden, they are giving time and attention to the personal injury victim.

DOCUMENTING YOUR DAMAGES

In calculating your economic damages, you have to take into account your lost wages, all your medical bills and medical treatment costs, and your future medical costs. To do this, you can't allow yourself to fall into the hands of a conservative, defense-oriented doctor. There are doctors who will screw you out of your case.

Some doctors have an internal prejudice against patients injured in an automobile accident who are seeking a legal settlement. They have a natural distrust for these patients because the doctors see these patients in the same light that they see people who sue for medical malpractice. They don't like litigious people, and by dint of you being involved in an auto accident, they put you in this category. They have no *rachmones* (a Yiddish word meaning compassion or empathy) for you.

You have to be aware that doctors like this exist. I know several. Every single person who comes into the office on a workers' compensation case gets sent back to work by their doctor. Oh, you've got a sprained wrist? Go back to work. You broke your arm? Go back to work. You've got a herniated disk in your back and you can't feel your toes? Go back to work.

Insurance companies and defense attorneys love doctors like this, and they send as many people their way as they can. These doctors who have a natural inclination to be overly conservative and suspicious of anyone injured in a work accident, auto accident, or slip-and-fall accident eventually find a niche doing medical exams for insurance companies. These doctors make big financial gains by being this way.

The insurance company can send you for what they call a compulsory medical exam (CME). Sometimes these are called defense medical exams (DMEs), and sometimes they are wrongly called an "independent" medical exam

(IME). That last term is completely misleading because these exams are hardly independent. The insurance company is paying a doctor to examine you and tell them what's wrong with you, and crazily enough, these doctors never find a whole lot wrong. The insurance companies pay these doctors well for these exams. The doctors have a lucrative niche, colluding with big insurance to cheat you out of the compensation you deserve.

Before choosing any doctor, make sure that physician is not on the insurance compulsory exam shortlist. These doctors are paid huge sums to do hundreds of exams each year on plaintiffs and provide a report on whether the injury was caused by the accident. I've seen the damage they can do.

In one case, I represented a thirty-two-year-old English teacher and soccer coach at our local high school. He rode his bike to school each morning. After school, he would exercise by riding his bike another ten to twenty miles. He was in great shape and felt like he was on top of the world.

One day, an eighty-three-year-old woman didn't see him and slammed into him, even though he was in the bike lane. He flew off his bike and landed on his head, neck, and shoulder and then onto his backside. He eventually needed neck surgery and three shoulder surgeries, but the CME doctor who examined him reported that my client's need for surgery was caused by the damage he suffered playing football fifteen years earlier, not from being run over by a car.

When I took his deposition, the doctor admitted that the year before, he was paid $450,000 by the old lady's insurance company to do a bunch of these exams. We eventually won that teacher a lot of money, but the case is a typical example of how disingenuous these CME doctors can be. Since they do not offer the plaintiff any advice or treatment, they do not suffer any malpractice risk. Every plaintiff lawyer knows the shortlist of these insurance doctors in their community. Make sure you are not using one of them. If you are not sure, call the doctor's office before you start treating and ask, "Is your doctor employed to investigate injuries for the insurance company? He may be doing IMEs (independent medical exams), DMEs (defense medical exams), or CMEs (compulsory medical exams)."

There are ways to defend yourself in a situation like this. One thing we do when a client is scheduled for a medical exam by the insurance doctor is that we'll schedule a medical exam with our own doctor right before the insurance exam. Our doctor finds that you have spasms, radicular complaints on your right side, a pain level of six out of ten, and that you have headaches and memory deficits. The insurance doctor finds none of this. They are both IMEs, but one doctor agrees with everything in the medical notes and decides that you're badly hurt, and the other doctor finds nothing and says you aren't. You can use your own IME to give yourself evidence and shore up your side of the argument. You may never go to court, but you are protecting yourself.

THE TESTS YOU NEED

Many auto accident injury cases turn on the results of key medical tests. The gold standard for many injuries is MRI, or magnetic resonance imaging. An MRI uses a magnetic field and computer-generated radio waves to create detailed images of the organs and soft tissues in your body. This includes the spine and the intervertebral disks; the joints, such as knees, shoulders, and hips; and other parts of the body that are now getting more visible on MRI. There are some special MRIs called diffuse tensor imaging MRI for brain injury (DTI/MRI) and new PET scan plus MRI combination tests that reveal all sorts of interesting unique things. MRIs use magnetism to create the scan, so there is no radiation, ill effect, or pain on the body.

X-rays, meanwhile, show hard-tissue damage, such as broken or misaligned bones. X-rays are now inexpensive, digital, and use far less radiation than they once did. If you have a neck injury, an X-ray might show that you've lost the natural curvature of your neck. With this condition, called loss of lordosis, your neck is unnaturally straight. If you lose that curvature, it's an indication your neck muscles are in spasm. The muscles are tightening up to avoid injury, and that's an objective finding because it's not something you can control and it's a clear sign of pain and injury.

In addition to the loss of lordosis and broken bones, X-rays can also reveal dislocated joints, bone fragments, and some internal injuries. But X-rays are limited in what they show.

The MRI will show more than a simple X-ray. It's used so often in auto accident cases because it shows soft tissue and spinal disks. The test works because every cell in your body has a positive and negative pole, and as you lie in the magnetic field of an MRI machine, the normal cells line up whereas diseased or injured cells do not. The radiofrequency waves generate the images.

Although insurance companies love to claim that your injuries came before or after your auto accident, MRIs are the only quality tool the plaintiff has to prove causation of injury to soft tissue affected in the accident. A properly placed MRI with good medical treatment and clinical correlation can show that your injuries were a direct result of the accident, and this can considerably strengthen your case if the MRI is used in conjunction with an accident report that documents the angle and speed of the crash you were involved in. MRIs also give doctors the information they need to treat you. Remember, auto accidents frequently cause unseen damage and micro-injuries that often aren't immediately apparent. MRIs can even show if pain or numbness for an injury has radiated to another part of your body.

In addition to herniated or injured disks, MRIs also reveal torn tendons, muscle tears, cartilage damage, organ injuries, and soft tissue damage that won't appear on an X-ray. Your doctor might order a CT scan, whose 3D view of the body is better than an X-ray and cheaper than an MRI but lacks the detail you'd get from an MRI.

Doctors often wait a few weeks before ordering an MRI so that damage from an accident has time to emerge and become detectable. In the meantime, it's wise to get your doctor to make a note in your medical records that he suspects a problem and wants to purposely delay an MRI exam to give the problem time to become apparent. This way, if your MRI does reveal a problem weeks later, the at-fault insurance company adjuster can't dismiss the result and claim you must have been injured sometime after the accident.

An early MRI can actually hurt your case. For example, if you have a tear in the annulus of your disk, the inside of your disk known as the nucleus pulposus probably has not leaked through the annulus fibrosis to show the protrusion of this material into the spinal area. You're not going to see that injury right after the accident, so if you had an MRI right away, it wouldn't show this injury. The other driver's insurance company could jump on that and say you weren't hurt, and if the case goes to trial, the jury might say the same thing.

A good doctor will know this and advise you to hold off for a few weeks. That way, you'll have an MRI that clearly shows the injury, and you won't have an MRI that doesn't show it. You won't have to explain away that early MRI.

TRAUMATIC BRAIN INJURIES

The term *mild traumatic brain injury* is the most absurd language usage since jumbo shrimp. Mild traumatic brain injury is anything but mild. The smallest brain injury can disable a person for life. If you are concerned about your brain after an accident, you should get tested for a brain injury. To figure this out, look at your mood and disposition; are you experiencing persistent debilitating headaches, dizziness, loss of your sense of humor, developing a new edginess, and having mental fogginess. Brain injuries must be documented over time. You must encourage your wife, husband, children, or best friend to share their observations with you. You may be aware of a change in your affect, but you'll likely attribute it to your physical pain and not a brain injury. You need to give your loved ones a checklist and say, "Tell me if any of these things are going on." We have provided an extensive checklist in the appendix.

You also must document this brain injury. Tell your doctor about any concerning symptoms. Let him know when your wife says she can't stand to live with you anymore because you snap for no reason and you've lost your sense of humor. Or you can have your spouse or partner come into the doctor's office with you and explain what's going on. The point is, you need to make this part of your medical record. This is an injury that wasn't your fault, and just like a physical injury, you deserve compensation for it.

When you have this suspected brain injury, you can get a referral to a neuropsychologist or a neurologist. These specialists can conduct neuropsychological testing and uncover the damage. If they also suspect a brain injury, they can order further neural brain testing. This testing is not inexpensive, but it is necessary to prove a significant brain injury. They are also developing more sophisticated tests, such as the PET scan or a SPEC scan DPI MRI combo, which allows doctors to see in real time how your brain is reacting to the stimuli. That technology is only available in about ten cities in the country.

Sadly, there is an epidemic of brain injury in this country that we don't diagnose. According to one report I read, about 1.7 million people suffer a traumatic brain injury every year, many of them from auto accidents. Mild brain injury is the most ubiquitous and least diagnosed injuries in the world of motor vehicles. There is a real need for quick, accurate, and reliable tests to detect these brain injuries.

Most of these injuries will heal. People also learn to live with it and start to overcome their injuries by creating new neurons to compensate. It self-corrects.

Still, the injury was there at one time, and many accident victims don't bring it up because they don't have any documentation. But it would add value to your case if you talk about it and see doctors who can diagnose it and make it a part of your medical records.

All of this is to say that if you are trying to settle your own auto accident case without a lawyer, you have to be aware of the possibility you may have suffered a traumatic brain injury. If you did, the case might be bigger than you realized, and you may need a lawyer. If you've suffered a traumatic brain injury, any settlement for less than $100,000 is inadequate, and you may not be able to get a better settlement without some help.

Say you are injured in an accident, and the at-fault driver carries $100,000 in bodily injury liability. You suspect you have a traumatic brain injury, but the adjuster is offering $7,500 to settle. You should get a lawyer and try to get $75,000 or $100,000 from the insurance company.

Although the injury is real, it can be difficult to convince the insurance company or a jury that you deserve compensation for it. That's because a brain injury often is not physically painful. It doesn't express itself as pain. You still get to go shopping, and you still get to go to the movies with your wife, and you still get to live a life. It's hard to document what is really wrong, and because of that, it can be difficult to prove damages to a jury. Insurance companies know this and often won't give you fair compensation for that injury.

PAYING FOR YOUR MEDICAL BILLS

If you've been injured in an auto accident, you're probably going to start incurring medical costs immediately. To pay for those medical bills, you have to use the best insurance available to you, and that's not always your regular health insurance policy.

The first thing to look at is workers' compensation. If the accident occurred while you were on the job or doing something within the scope of your employment, you have to go through workers' comp first. Workers' comp is regulated by the state you live in, and the process can vary by state. But generally speaking, if the auto accident occurred while you were on the job and your employer carries workers' comp, you must act quickly. You have to report the accident, and your employer has to give you the proper paperwork and guidance, and he has to file a claim with the insurer right away. Meanwhile, you have to file a formal workers' comp claim.

Once your claim is filed, the insurer will either approve or deny a claim. If they approve it, they'll make you a payment offer. This offer is structured to cover your costs for medical bills, disability payments, and lost wages. This could be either a structured settlement or a lump sum settlement. If your claim is denied, you can ask the insurance company to reconsider and review the decision, or you can formally appeal the denial.

The next type of coverage to tap to cover your medical expenses is your own auto policy. Many states require drivers to carry PIP (personal injury protection) insurance or MedPay insurance, and you have to tap these first. It's usually easy to do this, but these funds usually run out pretty quickly, depending on the coverage required by your state. For instance, Florida mandates that you carry at least $10,000 in PIP insurance, but Oregon requires $15,000.

If you don't have PIP, you probably have MedPay insurance on your automobile policy. MedPay is just another type of insurance that pays for medical bills. This type of coverage can also run out fairly quickly if your injuries are severe.

If you don't have PIP or MedPay or when those coverages run out, then you turn to your personal health insurance policy to pay for your medical bills.

Some people have an emotional response to paying for their own medical expenses when they were not at fault. They stand on principle: They say to the other driver's insurance, "You caused my injuries, so you should pay for my treatment." That attitude is completely understandable, but 99.9 percent of the time, the other guy's insurance company won't pay for anything. They'll say, "We're going to wait until you tell us what your injuries are, and then we'll give you money to settle the case in one fell swoop. But we won't pay for your doctor bills as we go along." In most states, this is legally correct and the preferred way of handling claims.

Another way to pay your medical bills is to get your doctor to sign a letter of protection. Under this agreement, a doctor holds off charging you for their services until your case is settled, and you can pay them with money you receive from the other driver's insurance. The doctor has a lien on your case.

Another option, which I don't recommend, is to get a non-recourse advance on your case. Essentially, you borrow money to pay for all your medical bills, and you pay the lender back—with steep interest—after your case is settled.

Letters of protection are a double-edged sword. The other driver's insurance company sees this as a conspiracy between the patient and the doctor. They'll claim that the only reason your doctor is finding your injuries is that he has a financial stake in them. The insurance company can discredit your doctor's opinion by arguing that he's only doing it for the payday.

Another aspect of medical payments to remember is a federal law called the Employee Retirement Income Security Act (ERISA). This law was set up to protect employees' pension and retirement plans from risky investments by their employers. The law was extended to include employee health insurance, and what this means is that your employer and your health insurance plan get an automatic lien anytime the employee gets their medical care repaid by a third party.

Say you're hit by another driver, and you tap your own health insurance (called first-party insurance) to pay your medical bills. Then you get repaid by the at-fault driver's insurance (third-party insurance). ERISA ensures that you pay back the first-party money when you receive that third-party settlement. You don't get to double-dip. Your insurance company might negotiate with you on an ERISA lien but not a lot.

PRIOR INJURIES

Most of us have been injured at some point in our life, and we have the scars to show for it. Sometimes a car accident will aggravate one of these prior injuries.

That fresh injury should not be discounted just because of a previous incident. We call people in this situation eggshell plaintiffs because they were more likely to be injured than someone who didn't have this preexisting condition. But the law helps you in this respect.

In most states, there is a jury instruction that tells jurors they are not permitted by the instruction of the court to discount prior injury if they can't clearly differentiate it from the present injury. But that law doesn't prevent insurance companies from trying to discount it. They try to do that all the time. They'll claim you are trying to take advantage of the system and that the pain you're experiencing isn't their responsibility.

This is not true, and the insurance companies know it. But the dispute can arise, particularly if you've been injured in a low-impact accident. The insurance company will ask, "How could you possibly be injured in this accident? It occurred at such a low speed!"

Your response is to say you were injured because you are an eggshell. I had some underlying damage that wasn't affecting me at the time, but now that your client hit me, this underlying damage has been reactivated, and now I'm in great pain. I was sitting at the red light not needing surgery, and then your client bumped me, and now I need surgery. It's your responsibility.

For example, say you had a neck injury in 1995, but over the next twenty-five years, you adjusted to the point where you can play tennis, climb mountains, and go hiking with your family. You are enjoying life, and everything is great. And then you were in a parking lot when another driver backed out of a parking space and hit you in your driver's side door. Was it a high-speed accident? No. He probably was going only fifteen miles per hour when he hit you. But the impact knocked your head sideways, and the herniated disk you had back in 1995, which has been sitting there inert a tenth of a millimeter from your spine, has been jostled and enlarged due to the accident. Now that disk is sitting directly on your spinal cord, and it's burning your arm to the point where you feel like honeybees are stinging you on the three fingers between your middle finger and your pinkie. It hurts so bad you can't close your hand.

These prior injuries shouldn't hurt your case, and often they help you build your case. You had this injury from 1995, and even though the doctor recommended surgery at the time, you put it off and felt better after six months. But then you got hit by this other driver, and suddenly you need that surgery. If it weren't for this person backing into me, I wouldn't have needed it. Even though ninety-nine out of a hundred drivers would not have been injured in that parking lot accident, you were, and the other driver's insurance company has to take responsibility for that.

NONECONOMIC DAMAGES

Economic damages are not difficult to calculate. Sometimes we hire an expert to testify about the total economic damages in a case. This is not because the economic damages are hard to understand; it is because it is a great presentation to have an expert telling a jury what the case is worth. But consider this: if the kid next door throws a baseball through your prized, historic stained-glass window, your neighbor's insurance should cover the $10,000 cost of replacing it. If a drunk driver slams into an armored vehicle carrying the Picasso painting you own and destroys it, you deserve to get compensated the $100 million you paid for the painting. But as precious as those things are, they are not as precious as your health.

Noneconomic damages, such as emotional trauma, inconvenience, and loss of enjoyment in life, are not as easy to measure. Nevertheless, these damages are more significant than any economic issue. The law requires that you should also be fairly compensated for any loss of these noneconomic assets. The problem is that there is no firm price you can attach to those things.

When I ask prospective jurors what is the most valuable thing in their lives, I typically get one of two answers: my health or my family. I can ask fifty or sixty different people and get the same answers. When I do, I ask, "You mean no one owns an expensive watch? A nice car? No one owns anything that is more important than their health and happiness?" And the consensus is, "No. Nothing is more valuable than that."

So then I ask if they will be able to gauge the value of someone else's loss of enjoyment, inconvenience, and zest for life. Are you going to be able to evaluate that in the same significant way that you just articulated to me how important your health, happiness, and family are to you? Is there anyone here who is going to object to judging the value of all that? Because that's the biggest number in all this.

A lot of people are uncomfortable with that, and I want to know who those people are so I don't put them on my jury. I want someone who feels like they can place a value on these noneconomic damages and who understands that it's a high-value item. I want people who understand that this economic shit is small. I don't want them to be bound by it. I don't want them to be anchored by the economic damages. I want them to give me multiples of those economic damages to cover the emotional damages that interfere with the things we value most in our lives.

If your accident has riven your psyche and erased your sense of well-being, you should be aware that you likely will not get a fair settlement from an adjuster. It may not be worth even trying to settle it yourself. You will never get enough money. It's almost impossible to make this demand yourself without sounding like you're exaggerating your symptoms or just trying to hit the lottery. Most people will sound like they are just bitching and moaning, and frankly, that is unattractive. It's also true that people tend to downplay their own injuries a lot. They have a hard time saying, "I'm hurt. Help me." It's hard enough for them to sell the economic package.

I would like to simply say you need an advocate, someone who can make the case for you. This is a much better place emotionally for you and others involved in the case. But even with that, in a presuit environment, emotional and noneconomic damages are simply underpaid. It is only when the jury hears about your life from you, your partner, or your child, parent, or coworker that the value of that life comes to light.

Whatever your circumstances, it's always vital that you protect yourself. If you are pursuing your own insurance settlement after a motor vehicle accident, you'll also need to sharpen your skills when it comes to negotiating with a claims adjuster. In the next chapter, we'll get you ready for that all-important step.

CHAPTER FIVE

———

NEGOTIATING YOUR CASE

Ten years ago, insurance adjusters were trained to evaluate injury claims according to the three legs of a three-legged stool. They looked at:

Liability. Who was at fault, or how much did each driver contribute to the accident? Most of the time, insurance adjusters have evidence—photos, witness statements, videos, statements from the two drivers, and police reports—that they use to make a determination.

Damages. How badly was someone hurt? Damages are split between economic damages and noneconomic damages, and the economic damages are comprised of medical expenses, lost wages, ambulance bills, diagnostic testing, surgery costs, rehabilitation, and postsurgical care, future nursing care, and physical therapy. There is a whole host of potential damages, and sometimes the total damages can get quite high. In states that have personal injury protection (PIP) insurance, this calculation is highly significant because, as we noted in our last chapter, plaintiff damages in some states have to reach a certain threshold before the plaintiff can sue the at-fault driver.

Coverage. How much insurance does the at-fault driver have? What kind of insurance and how much does the injured driver have?

When all these factors are added up, the at-fault driver's insurance adjuster will determine the best course of action to get the case settled for as little money as possible. Then they'll go to their supervisor and say, "This is a $150,000 accident. There are a half-million dollars in insurance, and I think I can get this settled for $50,000 to $112,000, and that's the authority I want on it." At this point, based on the adjuster's recommendation, the insurance company sets what's called a reserve. The reserve is just a quick and dirty estimate of what this case is likely to cost the insurance company.

Drivers who have been hit must remember that they have only about fifteen days to report anything new that might affect that reserve. You must let the other driver's insurance company know if an injury is more serious than you initially understood it to be or that the body shop expert discovered additional damage to your car. That fifteen-day period is followed by another period of sixty to ninety days when you can still report expenses that might affect that reserve. After six months, it's very difficult to get the insurance company to change that reserve number.

Don't be afraid to give the other driver's adjuster information. Let them know every truthful and helpful thing that shows how badly you were hurt or how much economic damages you suffered. If you find out from Facebook that the driver who hit you had brain surgery a month ago, tell the adjuster. They want to know as much as they can because one thing they truly hate is uncertainty and surprises. They want to avoid an award that's higher than the policy limit. And from your standpoint, you want to feed them information early; even though they won't tell you what the reserve is on a case, you want to do whatever you can from the outset to encourage them to set a high reserve.

For instance, I have a client named Fabrizzio, who was just hit in a rear-end collision. He sent me photos, and it doesn't look like much of an accident. Neither car shows much damage, and an insurance adjuster is likely to set a low reserve for a case like this.

But there are actually a couple of factors that make this a

much bigger case. For starters, if you look closely at the accident photos, you can see that a trailer hitch on the back of my client's car was bent up in the accident. That indicates that the at-fault driver struck my client with quite a bit of force. It takes a tremendous amount of force to bend a trailer hitch, and the hitch may have prevented much more dramatic damage to the back of Fabrizzio's vehicle.

More importantly, the adjuster needs to know that my client is an eggshell client in that he has a preexisting condition that makes him far more vulnerable to an injury in an accident like this.

Fabrizzio was in a severe car accident in 2004 that required neck surgery. Unfortunately, one of the screws the doctors put in his neck broke in 2017. That's a very dangerous situation. A loose screw coming in contact with his spinal cord could leave him paralyzed. But his doctor advised him against surgery, saying the operation was riskier than just living with the broken screw. However, he was going to have to always use caution in his physical activities so that the broken screw never moved closer to his spine.

These are all things Fabrizzio needs to make sure the insurance adjuster is aware of as soon as possible. Even though the damage to his car may not look significant, the potential damage to his health could be highly significant. He will need certain diagnostic tests that other accident victims wouldn't need because they don't have a broken screw sitting next to their spinal column.

AI PROGRAMS REPLACING ADJUSTERS

Remember, I'm describing the process from ten years ago. Today, it's a little different.

Insurance companies now rely less on well-trained people weighing all the factors in an accident and more on artificial intelligence (AI) to determine how much a case is worth. Insurance companies still use human adjusters, but those adjusters have lost all authority to do anything. The modern-day adjuster is just a human conduit for a software program.

There are three AI systems in use by insurance companies today, but the most frequently used one is called Colossus. You feed it data, and it spits out outcomes. Colossus reviews data from your case but also looks at the whole schema of injuries in the world and all the past verdicts of similar cases over the years and decides what your claim is worth. And that's what the adjuster goes with.

Insurance companies will tell you that the Colossus number is not the final determination. Colossus just gives advice to the adjuster, they say. It's just another data point.

I disagree. I'm pretty sure the insurance companies are not

spending a fortune to run and feed an AI program just so they can double-check their math.

The reason insurance companies insist that their AI programs are merely advisory is because if they admitted it was definitive, then opposing parties would want to get into the program, see the calculations, and explore the backend of the system. If we don't have that ability, then we can't fight them on a bad faith claim.

For instance, say the insurance company argues that it wasn't negotiating in bad faith because it was just going by what Colossus told them. The computer concluded what the case was worth, and the adjusters followed that guidance. Colossus was calculating the outcome in good faith.

As the plaintiff's attorney, I could disagree. How do I know Colossus is operating in good faith? Prove it to me. Show me the backend of the system. Show me all your data, programming, and calculations because I don't trust Big Brother.

I've done this before, and this kind of showdown makes insurance companies go batshit crazy. We'll never give you our data, they say. We'll never let you see our programming. It's all confidential. It's proprietary. It's...it's...And by this point, the adjuster is jumping up and down, clenching his teeth, and going red in the face.

When this happens, most judges will say that the insurance company can't rely on Colossus to beat a bad faith case. You have to rely on human judgment, so you have to put an adjuster on the stand and have them explain why they did what they did. You can't rely on AI to justify your actions.

What does all this mean for someone who is trying to settle their own auto accident case without an attorney? It means you have to provide the data that's needed for Colossus or some other AI program to give you a better-than-average outcome. That means providing the at-fault driver's insurance adjuster everything:

· Repair costs with part numbers listed in detail and hours worked on the repair
· Medical bills, including every treatment date with the CPT codes for every single treatment and every doctor's visit
· Future medical costs, listed in detail, including the future costs of each part of the surgery
· Any lost-wage information, including your wage statements and tax returns

Every bit of information you provide will help Colossus spit out a decent offer. Do not be surprised if the offer goes up when a lawyer becomes involved. Having a lawyer is a factor for Colossus. You want to give it all to the adjuster so it can be fed into the computer program. The more data Colossus has, the more it increases the value of your case.

All of the information you collect will also go into your demand letter, which we'll discuss later in this chapter. When the at-fault adjuster receives your demand letter, he'll call you back and give you an offer. It's likely to be a low-ball offer, but this is your opportunity to discuss your accident with a human being and plead your case for a better offer.

Each insurance company behaves differently, but some insurance companies make a practice out of swooping in quickly after an accident and trying to settle the case with a low-ball offer. Some companies will do this if the driver hasn't gotten an attorney and the damages seem like they could fly out of control. So the adjuster will call and offer $5,000 or $10,000 to settle the claim. Sometimes it makes sense for you to accept that offer. But if you've been injured at all, you want to hold off until you've sought medical treatment and you understand how badly you've been hurt.

YOUR ROLE IMMEDIATELY AFTER AN ACCIDENT

As one of the drivers, you have to do many of the same things an adjuster for the at-fault driver is doing. You have to look at the same three legs of the stool—coverage, liability, and damages.

While the other driver's adjuster is investigating, you have to build your own case. You must take photos at the accident, get statements from witnesses as well as their contact information, and get the responding police officer to issue a ticket to the other driver. Talk to the driver and get them to apologize to you. If you can get them to apologize in a quick video, all the better. The more you can prove that someone else is 100 percent at fault, the stronger your case will be. If you were hit from behind because the driver was distracted by their phone, see if you can get them to admit that. This opens them up to punitive damages and enhances the value of the case.

You also need to call your own insurance company right away. They will want to discuss the property damage and get a statement from you proving that you were not at fault.

If the details or liability in your accident are in dispute, you may have to do some additional legwork. Were there any businesses nearby? Did someone see the accident occur? Did any of the nearby businesses have video surveillance at the time that may have caught your accident? Was there a video camera on the stoplight where the crash occurred? Do you need to file a request to review that video?

Your demand letter is the culmination of building your case. It's not something you sit down to write the evening of your accident. Instead, it's a compilation of all the communications and information you've sent the insurance adjuster in the days and weeks following your accident. Remember, you need to be continually feeding the adjuster information about your case so they can feed it to Colossus and increase the reserve.

Plan on sending the at-fault driver's adjuster an introductory letter within five days of the accident. That letter explains who you are, that you're injured, and whether you've been to the emergency room or doctor. So you might say, "Hi, my name is Brian. Here's the police report on the accident in which your client hit my car. I was not at fault, but I've been injured. I went to the hospital and learned that I broke my wrist. Also, my neck hurts, my back hurts, and a sore knee prevents me from walking or exercising. I'll be going to an orthopedist about that and to a podiatrist about a sharp pain I feel in my heel." You give the adjuster the name of all your doctors, promise to send them medical records as soon as you receive them, and invite them to contact you if they need additional information. See the appendix for this form letter.

At sixty days after your accident, you should send the adjuster an update. Send them any additional medical records and let them know how you continue to suffer from the accident. Inform them of upcoming medical needs that resulted from the accident. Enclose copies of all your medical bills and payments. Send them a log of what's been paid by the PIP insurance. Explain how you plan to pay for medical treatments after your PIP runs out. A similar form letter is included in the appendix.

At the same time as you are providing information, you are also asking for it. The third leg of the stool is collectability, so you need to be looking for whom you can collect from and letting them know that you will be collecting money from them. This likely includes your own insurance company. Everyone who is on your collectability list has to be given the ability to pay you when you ask, so you have to reach out to them. Giving them information is better than remaining silent.

THE DEMAND LETTER

Once you've set up your no-fault payments, seen the various doctors, and gathered the relevant medical reports and accident investigation documents, you're ready to prepare a demand letter to the other driver's insurance company. The demand letter is your ultimatum listing a factual summary of your claim, all the problems you experienced, and how much you want in compensation.

The factual summary will list all your minor and major injuries, physical damages, disfigurement, and emotional trauma you experienced as a result of the accident. You are making your case for compensation, so it's vital that you write it in a cogent, thorough, and well-organized fashion. Here are a few more things to consider.

SETTLEMENT NEGOTIATIONS ONLY

Make sure to include your name, address, and phone number, as well as your insurance company information, the adjuster, the claim number, and the date of the accident. You also want to make sure the letter is headed with a term such as *For Settlement Purposes Only*. That's vital because settlement negotiations are considered privileged and can't be used against you later.

For example, if you wrote a demand letter asking for $50,000, but later you wind up in a lawsuit asking for $1 million, the attorneys for the other side can't turn around and use that letter to undermine your case. They can't hold up your demand letter in front of a jury and say, "But Mr. Victim, last year you thought you needed only $50,000, and now you want a million. Are your injuries really that bad if all you wanted last year was $50,000?"

So make sure you indicate at the top of your letter that it is for settlement negotiations only. That protects you by notifying everyone that your intent is to keep the letter privileged.

EXPLAINING WHAT HAPPENED

The first paragraph of your demand letter is usually a summary: I was involved in an accident on the date above that was caused by your client. You also want to include anything that happened before or after the accident that helps put your claim in perspective. Include anything that is central to why you are damaged.

For instance, my client Fabrizzio's demand letter will certainly reveal that he needs special medical treatment because of the broken screw in his neck. Because he was in such a vulnerable condition when he was rear-ended, it's likely he'll need specialized care that another driver wouldn't require. All that should be described at the beginning of the letter so the adjuster understands certain demands or calculations we'll make in the rest of the letter.

LIABILITY

The next step in the demand letter is to establish liability. This is where you assign blame. You want to explain what happened in the accident and how the company's client is to blame. So you might say something like, "I was stopped at a red light in the southbound lane of Liberty Street at the intersection of Kuebler Drive. When the light turned green, I proceeded through the intersection. I was nearly through the intersection when your client ran a red light and struck the rear passenger-side panel of my Ford Taurus, causing extensive damage to my vehicle and causing my head to strike the window."

INJURIES AND MEDICAL TREATMENT

This section of the demand letter is where you detail your injuries and how doctors have treated you. You want to be sure to include every injury that has caused you physical or emotional pain. You want to document scarring or other disfigurements. You want to include all the doctors you saw and what you saw them for.

DAMAGES

This is the section where you lay out what you feel your settlement should be. The value of some of your damages will be clear cut, but others will be more subjective—and more likely to be disputed. You want your first demand to be as high as you can reasonably make it while giving yourself room to compromise on the amount. Making an exorbitant demand is counterproductive because it suggests that you aren't negotiating in good faith and that you don't have a good understanding of the process. Either way, you lose credibility with the adjuster, and this will hurt your chances of a successful negotiation.

There are three possible damage components you may want to include in your demand letter:

- Economic damages
- Noneconomic damages, such as pain and suffering
- Punitive damages

ECONOMIC DAMAGES

These are provable damages whose value is easy to calculate and document. In this section of the letter, include every medical expense, from the ambulance ride you needed to the ibuprofen you continue to take to manage swelling and lingering pain. Your goal here is to translate all the injuries and treatments you received into expenses so the adjuster can clearly see the correlation between injuries and damages.

You must record every single visit to the doctor, hospital, or urgent care facility, every physical therapy appointment, the cost of each diagnostic test. Go through each medical bill and list the treatment code for each visit, and include notes from the doctor. If you will need future treatment, make sure your doctor notes that in your file.

In addition to listing your previous medical expenses, you need to calculate what your future expenses will look like. For instance, if your doctor expects you to need palliative care that includes a series of six physical therapy visits and three separate periods of the year, you make the calculation: "I will need physical therapy eighteen times a year for the rest of my life. If I live to be sixty-five, that means I'll need thirty-one years of visits. At $100 per visit, that will cost $55,800."

Again, everything is fair game. Every Uber ride you take to a doctor's appointment is reimbursable. If you lost your $500 deposit on a cruise because you were too injured to go, that's reimbursable.

You also want to include lost wages in this section. This includes the time you spend at doctor's appointments and therapy sessions. So, in the example above, if a physical therapy appointment takes four hours and you go eighteen times a year for thirty-one years, and your hourly wage is $30, that's $66,960.

NONECONOMIC DAMAGES

Another portion of the damages section is for noneconomic damages, such as pain and suffering. This includes your mental anguish, inconvenience, loss of enjoyment in life, disfigurement, and physical impairment. These are all the factors that a jury would be asked to weigh your case.

How much do you ask for? There is no methodology that you have to stick to to decide on a number. You can make that number anything you want because a juror can make it anything they want. They're not bound by any number.

Years ago, the rule of thumb for noneconomic damages was three times your economic damages. You would take the value of your economic award, multiply it by three and subtract one-third, and what's left is your noneconomic award. More recently, noneconomic damages at trial have been coming in equal to the economic damages. If you're negotiating with an adjuster, they don't want to give you anything for pain and suffering. Oftentimes, their initial offer is even below your documented economic damages because they think doctors charge too much.

PUNITIVE DAMAGES

Under certain circumstances, the law entitles you to punitive, or consequential, damages. This occurs when the defendant was drunk or texting when they caused your injury accident. Punitive damages are really punishment damages. They must be requested after the judge has facts that show the defendant acted with an intentional desire to harm the plaintiff or that the defendant behaved with a reckless disregard for human safety. Punitive damages are awarded by a jury as a multiple of the economic and noneconomic damages after those damages are decided by the jury.

One time, we had to sue a nice kid named Alexander. He made a mistake and drove to his hotel after drinking too many beers. He didn't stop at a red light and hit the car in front of him, which was properly stopped at a red light. Alex was charged with DUI. We were not involved in the criminal case, but we sued him for the damages the wreck caused my client. We took Alex's deposition, and he admitted that he drank too many beers that night. That fact allowed us to ask the judge for permission to add in a punitive damage claim. The judge agreed that drunk driving was reckless conduct, and she added punitive damages to our case.

We took the case to trial. Our client was awarded $270,000 for all her economic and noneconomic damages. Then we asked the jury for punitive damages for three times the damages. The jury agreed, and they added another $540,000 to our case. The final judgment was over $700,000. The worst part of punitive damages for everyone is that insurance will not pay for them. The defendant must pay them, and the defendant can't discharge them in bankruptcy. That makes them awful for everyone. The bottom line: BEWARE punitive damages!

A basic draft demand letter is attached to the appendix at the end of the book.

DEMAND LETTER NEGOTIATIONS

It's crucial that you put a time limit on your demand letter. In our law office, we give the adjuster thirty days to respond, and you can ask them to get back to you in that time frame as well. That will give the adjuster time to review your case and get back to you with a counteroffer.

That counteroffer signals the start of the negotiation process. In all likelihood, the adjuster's counteroffer is going to be considerably lower than your initial offer. The best way to handle this is to tell the adjuster that you want to consult with your attorney or some other advisor and that you will get back to them. This gives you a little breathing room, but it also gives you the opportunity to talk the offer over with someone. That person could be an attorney, but it could also be your spouse, a friend, or a grandfather. Explain the situation to them and ask their help in formulating a counteroffer.

Your first step in the negotiating process is to set a range for a settlement. What's the best likely result, and what's the worst? Once you've determined that, determine what your minimum acceptable value will be. In other words, what "final offer" from the adjuster would convince you to break off negotiations and hire an attorney? This decision has to factor in the cost of hiring an attorney, the time involved, and the likely outcome if your case were to go to trial.

For example, say you were rear-ended by another driver on an exit ramp, leaving you with a neck injury that may not require surgery but will certainly require months of physical therapy. The other driver's bodily injury liability coverage is $100,000, and you know from your research that cases like this typically settle for $30,000. Your demand letter asks for $40,000, but the most the adjuster offers you is $5,000. Is it worth hiring an attorney? Absolutely. An attorney will get you at least the $30,000, which means that you walk away with a $20,000 settlement after the attorney's fees and expenses are deducted.

However, if the adjuster offers you $20,000—half of what you asked for—the math doesn't justify hiring an attorney. It would be a wash. In this scenario, $20,000 is the minimum acceptable value you use in negotiating with the adjuster. If the adjuster offers anything less than that, you can convincingly throw up your hands and let the adjuster know that an attorney will soon be taking over your case.

NEGOTIATION TACTICS

A good advisor will tell you that successful negotiation requires that both sides gain something and that both sides lose something. They will also advise you to stick to the facts. Many people think it's okay to use deception or trickery or poker-style bluffs to get what they want, but if a lawyer were negotiating, bar association rules would prevent them from making false or misleading statements during negotiations. Those techniques are unethical, and you should avoid them, too.

Instead, enter negotiations with a firm understanding of your case. Try to collect as much information about your case as you can, and look at your claim the way a juror might. Where is your case particularly strong? Where is it weak? Is there an emotional factor that might prompt a jury to deliver a large verdict or, conversely, to show sympathy for the defendant and return a lesser verdict? This will help you to know what to demand and what to concede—or when to break off negotiations altogether and hire an attorney.

There are some online resources that might help you put your case into perspective and help you determine its value. VerdictSearch, for instance, provides online tools (for a fee, although the company offers a free introductory trial offer) that help you estimate damages, analyze insurers' settlement offers in cases similar to yours, and even project the likelihood of you winning if your case went to trial. Thomson Reuters offers its Westlaw Edge service that helps you assess the value of your case and to evaluate whether the offer you get is reasonable.

Some people may feel like they've emptied their magazine in their demand letter and have little ammunition left for negotiating with the adjuster. However, the adjuster's response is going to give you fresh ammunition. In that response, the adjuster is likely to dispute some of your claims or the values you put on certain damages. So focus on those areas of disagreement and point out in future negotiations why the number the adjuster is using for a particular item is incorrect.

Remember, negotiation is really about resolving disputes, so identify those disputes and identify how much you are willing to compromise on each one. It's okay to have a winner-take-all mentality when you're at trial, but when negotiating with the adjuster, you will need to concede some things, and so will the insurance company. Most negotiations involve a series of mini negotiations on discrete areas of disagreements.

It helps if you can create an agenda that lists the areas of disagreement and prioritizes them. Studies have shown that negotiations are more effective when both sides agree on what the key issues are and how to discuss them.

According to James Alexander Tanford of the Indiana University School of Law, "successful bargaining occurs when you are prepared both to be cooperative and to demand cooperation from your opponent." One way to accomplish this is to respond to the adjuster's initial counteroffer with a letter that outlines the areas of disagreement and sets a proposed agenda and approach for discussing each one. When your next call starts, you can suggest that you and the adjuster follow your agenda. The adjuster will probably agree. Set a proposed time limit on your negotiating session and follow up on the session with a recap email that sets out what you agreed to and what you still must negotiate on.

As you go back and forth—whether it's on the phone with the adjuster or through written communications—the key is to remain professional. Be prepared to explain how you arrived at your numbers so that your settlement offer appears to be well reasoned and not arbitrary. It also helps if you personally and privately decide beforehand those issues on which you're willing to concede and those on which you intend to stand firm.

For example, say you were out of work for ten weeks. You calculate that at $40 per hour for forty hours a week with five hours of overtime each week that you are out $16,000 in regular pay and $3,000 in overtime pay. So you ask for $19,000. You might feel strongly about the regular pay but privately admit to yourself that you're willing to negotiate with the adjuster on the amount of overtime pay since that is speculative. If it's not speculative—if, for instance, you've earned the same amount of overtime during this time period every one of the last ten years—you need to show the adjuster your pay stubs from past years.

NEGOTIATING BEHAVIOR

It doesn't help to get emotional during negotiations. The adjuster is not treating this as an emotional issue—it's just another assignment for them—and the adjuster will see anger or tears as a sign that your emotions are driving your settlement offer and not the dispassionate calculations that insurance companies respect so much. So tamp down your emotions and remain straightforward, thorough, and persistent. When you allow emotion to enter the negotiations, the adjuster knows he's winning the argument. Treat the whole thing as a business transaction.

That said, cooperation is key. Both sides must be willing to give a little. If the adjuster isn't offering any concessions, point that out.

I am a huge Chris Voss fan. Voss was a chief negotiator for the FBI for many years. He has broken down some verbal cues in negotiations to help people become more effective negotiators. The first verbal trick is to talk like a "late-night DJ voice," using your lowest and most calm voice. Just speaking low and slow will help put the adjuster at ease.

The second trick is to call a label. Labels are verbal observations that point out an observed emotional display. You start a sentence by saying, "It seems like..." or "It looks like..." or "It feels like..." and then laying the behavior at your opponent's feet. Using a label can help you overcome whatever the other side is *not telling you about why they are not presenting a fair offer*. For example: *It seems like you don't have the authority to actually make a decision on this file. Is there's a supervisor or someone who will come down on you?*

Third, you will be surprised how far using a mirror will get you. Mirrors are simple. You just mimic the other side in the way you communicate. This can be as simple as using the same body language if you are able to see each other or saying the last few words in a tone similar to the speaker's. Say the mirror back in a question format, so your tone is attentive and not aggressive. You're simply listening attentively and reflecting on their words.

Here is another big point for me: I had no clue how hard it was to get people to say yes. Saying yes makes people uncomfortable. Saying no makes people feel protected. Use this bit of knowledge by phrasing your questions in a no format. By doing this, you create the illusion that the other side is in control. You can ask, "Are you not able to make a deal and get this case settled?" "Are you trying to avoid a settlement?"

The last verbal trick is to go negative on your side so the other side can't put your negative points on you. Take them off the table early. It is a way to set the adjuster up for a negotiation. Say something like this at the start of your negotiation: "It probably looks like I am being unrealistic asking for $100,000, but I believe this is a fair settlement offer." This verbal trick will help you move the adjuster toward a better resolution of your case.

In the end, one of your best leverages with the adjuster is reminding him that you could still go and get a lawyer. The adjuster doesn't want to hear that. If you get a lawyer to represent you, the insurance company is going to pay a lot more than they will by fairly negotiating directly with you. What's more, with a lawyer, the possibility exists that the case will go to trial, and the insurance company doesn't want that either. A trial could result in a large jury verdict—something that makes insurance actuaries punch out their adding machines. I am sure they will say something to the effect of "Well, if you do that, the offer won't change, and you will be splitting the same money with the lawyer."

The key is getting the adjuster to respect that you know what you're doing. You've read the book on how to do this. You understand your case, and you understand how insurance works. You want the adjuster to think that you're getting advice from a lawyer because you're treating the negotiation the way a lawyer would treat it. Allow the adjuster to feel the slight pressure and uncertainty that comes from knowing this could wind up in a lawsuit.

WHAT TO AVOID

The biggest mistake people make when negotiating their own insurance settlement is to not get proper medical treatment. They downplay and undervalue their injuries by not understanding what's happening to them medically and what kind of problems they might develop in the future.

Again, it's crucial that you properly document your injuries. You must do this immediately. One thing a good lawyer will bring to your case is an understanding of how to develop that medical documentation correctly.

Another mistake is allowing your negotiations with the adjuster to go on too long. Negotiations can last as long as you allow, and as we mentioned earlier, the insurance industry is happy to keep your money as long as they can so they can continue earning on the investment they have it in. You must keep in mind that there is a statute of limitations on personal injury cases. It varies from two to six years, depending on the state you live in. So you have to keep your eye on that date so your negotiations don't stretch beyond that and you wind up not getting anything.

Try to get the negotiations over as quickly as possible. Go in with clear goals and a timetable, and understand that you aren't going to get full value for your case. Understand what you are willing to settle for and try to get the adjuster there as quickly as possible.

The worst thing you can do is fail to keep good records of your expenses. Every doctor's appointment, every parking meter, every aspirin purchase must be recorded, and you have to hold on to the receipt. You must have data, and you must have proof. If you don't, it's like it didn't happen.

You also need the right doctor. Some doctors are very good at documenting your injuries and making sure you see all the specialists you need. Other doctors are less sympathetic; they hate lawyers, they hate plaintiffs, and they refuse to see possible complications from your injuries. As we mentioned in an earlier chapter, they are conservative by nature, and they can really hurt your case. Orthopedists tend to be this way, and so are a lot of neurosurgeons, hospitalists, emergency room doctors, and podiatrists.

How do you find the right doctor? I would suggest you contact a couple of local plaintiff lawyers and ask for a recommendation. Just tell them that you've been in an accident, but before you hire an attorney, you want to set up the medical claim. Ask them to recommend a doctor who will be sympathetic to your situation. Most offices will be glad to help you. Every referral helps, and doctor referrals are great for the lawyer, the doctors, and the patient.

OTHER NEGOTIATIONS

In building your case for an insurance settlement, you may also need to negotiate with your doctors.

For example, if you have used up all your PIP and you need to use your regular health insurance to pay for surgery, it might make sense for you to ask the doctor not to bill your insurance. Instead, ask them to do the surgery under what's called a letter of protection. Basically, this letter says that the surgeon will take payment after your personal injury case is settled rather than to get paid under your health insurance policy.

Say you need a $100,000 surgery. If you were to get it under your health insurance, your doctor would likely have a contract with your insurance that pays him a predetermined amount. Let's say it is $44,000 for that particular surgery.

Many health insurance companies have a provision in their health insurance contract with the patient that says they don't need to pay for a medical procedure if it can be paid for by the proceeds of an injury case. That means the injury case is supposed to pay for that surgery. Other health policies pay for the medical treatment but demand to be repaid when the patient gets settlement money.

However, if the health insurance won't cover the surgery or treatment, the patient can ask the doctor to complete the treatment and also give a lien against the future injury settlement. That lien is commonly called a letter of protection, or a LOP. By holding a LOP, the surgery is completed with $100,000 price tag. That is the real cost of the surgery according to the doctor's price list, also called a charge master. The patient can use that $100,000 bill to set a high bar for the defendant's auto insurance adjuster regarding the damages the defendant owes to the plaintiff. Because the surgery was not paid for by a health insurance company, it is valued at $56,000 more, and therefore the defendant's insurance adjuster needs to give you more money to settle the case. They can't argue that the actual cost of the surgery was $44,000 and not $100,000 because the plaintiff actually owes $100,000.

Then, once you come to a settlement amount, you are permitted to return to the doctor and negotiate how much you will pay for that surgery. Will you pay $90,000 or $45,000 or some amount in between? That is a question that can't be answered in this book, except to say that no professional in this entire equation believes you will ever pay the doctor $100,000—not the doctor, lawyers, or insurance adjusters. This is simply how medical costs are negotiated in car accident cases. The good thing is that if you are working with a doctor you know, you can usually convince them to not charge you more than twice the Medicare rate, or 65 percent of the total bill. Some doctors even cut their fees down to Medicare rates just to help their patients pay the bills.

Bear in mind that negotiating your own insurance settlement will take some time. Some of the steps may seem complicated, but the process itself is usually straightforward and manageable. The key is to stay focused and, when uncertain, to ask questions.

Still, some folks may look at the process and decide that

it's too much for them. At that point, they'll need to find an attorney. That, too, can be a challenging process. But in the next chapter, we'll map out for you how to find an attorney who can do the job for you.

CHAPTER SIX

FINDING THE RIGHT REPRESENTATION

A woman named Joanne recently called me about her case. Joanne was T-boned by another vehicle at an intersection in Jupiter, Florida. She was pulling out of a parking lot onto the main thoroughfare when another driver blew through a red light and struck Joanne in the front passenger-side quarter panel and spun her car around.

Joanne went to the hospital, and the other driver, a twenty-four-year-old single mom, also suffered minor injuries and went to the hospital. The young mother didn't notice the red light because she was feeding her child yogurt at the time. She steered with her left hand while she twisted around to spoon-feed her child with her right. She was looking backward when she went through the red light at 50 mph and crushed Joanne's car.

At the hospital, Joanne felt sorry for the other driver. She saw her there with her child and decided that she did not want to bring an action against her.

Joanne was still feeling beat up after being treated at the hospital and went to her doctor. Her own insurance company told her that her personal injury protection (PIP) insurance would pay for her doctor bills and that she had MedPay, which would cover another $5,000 on top of her PIP. Joanne felt reassured that she would not be stuck with any outstanding medical bills.

Despite feeling a bit sore, Joanne returned to work. The other driver's insurance company contacted her and asked how she was feeling. They sounded genuinely concerned. Joanne told the adjuster that she was not "one of those sue-happy people," but the adjuster said she wanted to ensure Joanne would not have to come out of pocket for her medical care. That's nice, Joanne thought. The adjuster said she wanted to give Joanne $5,000 if Joanne would sign a release. Joanne agreed. She signed the release, cashed the check, and came away feeling like this would resolve the issue.

But Joanne's aches and pains worsened in the coming

weeks. About a month after signing the release, she learned that she was going to need neck surgery. The $5,000 she settled for was not going to cover the expense.

Joanne called the adjuster and explained the situation. The neck surgery was going to cost over $100,000. She would be out of work for eight weeks. She needed help. Things had changed, and she needed to reopen her claim.

This time, the adjuster didn't sound so nice. Sorry, Joanne. You signed a release. The claim is closed.

Horrified, Joanne called our office. She thought the $5,000 payment was just to cover any medical expenses her own insurance did pay for, she said. She had no clue this was the final settlement. Could she give back the $5,000 and get the release overturned?

Sadly, the answer was no. Joanne was out of luck. The release she signed caused her to lose her rights against the defendant, and because she settled the case without checking with her own insurance first, Joanne lost the right to collect her own underinsured motorist benefits.

It was, by any measure, the worst possible outcome. Joanne's case was probably worth $500,000 to $1,000,000 or more depending on the medical outcome, but Joanne was left with just $5,000.

Joanne's case illustrates what can happen if you are seriously injured in an accident that's not your fault and you fail to get proper legal help. Joanne didn't understand the seriousness of her accident. She didn't understand the different policies she could tap. She didn't fully understand her medical condition before settling. She didn't think about how much work she would miss or what medical complications might surface in the future. She didn't do any of the things necessary to decide whether she needed an attorney to help her settle her case. If she had known the damage she suffered would be over $500,000, would she still be one of "those people" who won't want to sue?

Although this book will help you settle your own personal injury insurance claim when you've been in a typical run-of-the-mill auto accident, some accidents are serious enough to warrant getting an attorney to represent you. A good, experienced attorney will make sure you set your case up right from the start, getting the right medical treatment, and properly documenting your injuries. An attorney will always get you more for your case than you can get on your own.

But how do you find this person?

LOOKING FOR THE RIGHT LAWYER

Most people who are looking for legal representation do one

of two things: they ask friends and family to refer someone, or they go online and read attorneys' websites to find someone who has the experience and expertise to help.

Neither of these approaches is particularly good. For one thing, there is simply too much misleading or worthless information on the internet that it's hard to distinguish between experienced, honest attorneys and unskilled lawyers with exaggerated credentials. A much better approach is to ask another personal injury lawyer whom they would hire to represent them. Of course, you can't call a local personal injury lawyer for that kind of advice—they will either try to get your case themselves, or they might be insulted and uncooperative as a result.

Instead, contact someone in a different city. They would not be taking your case themselves because it's outside their normal jurisdiction. But they know all the great lawyers in the state. So ask that lawyer for three potential candidates, and then you do your background check on those three and pick the one that seems best for you. Once you've done that, ask the lawyer you consulted to call this person and introduce you to them. That way, the attorney you consulted gets a 25 percent referral fee—which comes out of your attorney's portion of your settlement and not yours—and you get the inside track on great representation.

If you have a garden-variety auto accident case, any one

of these three attorneys will serve you well. Just pick one and go.

But if your case is more complicated and has a higher value, you could take the time to meet individually with each one. Ask about their office structure. How much time will the attorney spend on the case, and how much of it will be handled by paralegals? What kind of outcome has the attorney had with cases similar to yours? What's the typical timeline for settling cases like yours? What percentage of this attorney's cases wind up in trial, and how many are settled before trial? How often does this attorney take a case to trial? If your case involves any special circumstances, will the attorney consult with other legal experts? If your case is complicated and will require a big investment for expert witnesses or trial preparation, does this attorney's firm have the resources to handle that expense?

Just as important as these questions you ask your attorney is the central question you have to ask yourself: What do I want out of this case?

Most clients fall into two camps. About 90 percent of clients simply want a settlement. They want to be compensated fairly as quickly as possible. A much smaller percentage is more interested in justice. They want their day in court. They want an opportunity to tell their story to a jury and to have that jury tell them how much their case is worth.

If you fall into that latter camp, it's crucial that you let your lawyer know. If your lawyer knows this, she won't waste time on prelitigation and negotiations and will instead focus on building your case for trial. Your lawyer may also disagree with you about taking the case to trial and decline to take your case as a result.

By the same token, if you have expectations for a specific settlement, you also need to let your attorney know. You may want $1 million for your injury, but your attorney may think it's worth only $100,000. When that happens, you either have to adjust your expectations or go out and find an attorney who agrees with you. We have had potential clients come in who say they want $1 million. But when I look at their case, I can see right away that it's actually worth much less. So I'll tell the client, "I don't think your injured toe is worth $1 million. I don't think I can sell that to a jury. If you feel you must get $1 million out of this case, you need to get a different lawyer."

EXTRA LEGAL HELP

If your case is particularly unusual, you must understand that your attorney may need to consult with other attorneys with a particular expertise. This may cut into the size of your settlement, but it's often worth the extra expense. Most of the time, the attorney will earn back every penny you are paying them and more.

For example, I was recently contacted by a lawyer representing a driver who was struck by a train. The driver had approached a railroad crossing. The gates were up, and the lights were not flashing, so the client proceeded to cross the tracks. An oncoming train traveling at full speed struck the car right behind the driver's door. The driver survived but suffered partial paralysis and some brain damage.

The lawyer who called me said he'd gotten a $3 million settlement offer from the insurance company. Did I think that was a fair settlement?

Three million dollars is nothing to sneeze at. But I told this lawyer that railroad cases are complex and required special experience and knowledge. I happened to know a third lawyer who'd handled a lot of railroad cases. I advised the attorney to contact my friend in Jacksonville. He'll look the case over, I said, and if he can drive more value into it, he'll let you know. My friend eventually joined the case as co-counsel, and the two lawyers settled the case for $8.2 million a few weeks later.

As you can see from that story, expertise matters! If you're in a serious accident with a commercial truck and you come to my law firm for help, I will take that case and maximize the value by co-counseling with one of three major trucking lawyers in the United States. They don't practice in Florida, but they can act as my expert to set up the case for maximum value. I know who specializes in truck cases, and I know they will work with me to bring huge value to those cases. If it is a motorcycle case, my partner is one of the best of the best. If it is a maritime case, my other partner is one of the few true specialists. But if you bring us a medical negligence or nursing home negligence or sexual assault case, or even a first-party homeowner's hurricane case, we do not have the best talent here to help you, so we will find them for you and make the introduction.

Most attorneys won't bring on other attorneys, however. They will try to keep the case for themselves, and you'll miss out on a larger settlement as a result. That is a bad decision. It is better to do the case exceptionally well and get your share of the most money.

GET SOMEONE WITH A GOOD TRACK RECORD

Even if you're not the kind of plaintiff who wants their day in court, it's wise to hire an attorney who has routinely taken cases to court. If you hire a personal injury lawyer who rarely takes a case to trial, you are hiring someone who is willing to take less than full value on their cases. However, if you hire someone who goes to trial two or three times a year and often emerges victorious, this makes insurance companies edgy and more likely to offer you a good settlement without a trial.

Here's why: Insurance companies hate the unknown. Trials

are the unknown. For an insurance company, trials are a deep black pool, and the insurance company doesn't know what's hidden beneath the surface. They do not want to see a runaway verdict on their case, and they are willing to pay you top dollar if they see that your lawyer has a history of effectively taking cases to trial and forcing insurers to jump in that pool. As a result, attorneys who don't hesitate to take a case to trial can get a better deal for their clients than an attorney who never goes to trial.

And, really, a fair deal is all most clients want. Most are not interested in the risk involved with a jury. A jury can get you twice the settlement if you can convince them. But it can also give you much less. The jury may not like you as a witness. You may not testify in a clear way, or you may come across as greedy or unpleasant. I've had clients get on the stand and shrink and admit fault. I've had clients get unexpectedly aggressive. People are not used to performing, and crazy things can happen. This is why we built a mock courtroom in my office. It's not so the attorneys can practice; it's so plaintiffs can get some practice.

Here's an example. I had one client who was injured when she slipped on a wet floor, leaving a Walmart. There had been a thunderstorm while she was inside shopping, and the store's entrance-exit areas were all wet. The store had set up warning signs, but they were all facing outward for people entering the store. My client was leaving and didn't get the warning. She slipped and fell and fractured her coccyx.

Walmart refused to pay, so we went to trial. The day before the trial started, we met with our client to talk over her testimony—how she fell, why, the doctors she saw, the injury she suffered, the expenses she incurred as a result, and all the other aspects of her case.

Our client was very nervous. That wasn't surprising because a lot of people will be nervous testifying before a jury. It's a lot of pressure. So we reassured her.

One of the questions we rehearsed had to do with how much she was responsible for the accident. We wanted her to be likable, so we asked her, "What percentage are you at fault for this accident? Do you take any responsibility for not seeing the wet floor signs?" And she was honest in her answer. "If I had not been trying to manage my packages and eager to get out to my car, I might have been more attentive," she said. "It's possible I would have seen the signs and the wet floor and used more caution, but I was struggling with my packages, and by the time I saw the outward-facing signs, I was already falling. So I would say I was between 12 percent and 20 percent responsible."

We practiced that question and answered twenty times.

The next day at trial, we asked her, "Maria, do you think you are in any way at fault in this accident?"

"Yes. Yes, I'm at fault."

"Well, how much are you at fault?"

Maria went white. Ghost white. "No, I'm at fault. It's my fault."

We tried a few more times to corral our client and get her to accept only a portion of the blame, but she had completely lost her composure and just couldn't come around. She persisted that she was at fault. She settled on that conclusion and couldn't seem to budge from it.

On cross-examination, Walmart's defense attorney capitalized. "We understand this is stressful," he said. "Take a deep breath. It's okay. We know that the truth often comes out when people take the stand. You just admitted that you're at fault for this accident. You know in your heart of hearts that you're to blame for this accident, correct?"

"Yes," our client said. "I am at fault."

Our case was toast. We got zero.

I vowed to never let that happen to me again. I would never

let a client go to trial without some experience testifying in a courtroom. At first, we tried to rent courtrooms from the county, and when we learned they wouldn't allow that, we built our own.

The point here is that you never know what will happen in a trial. The defense won that case, but it was just as likely that if my client had testified truthfully, the verdict could have gone in a different direction.

There are other reasons why you should try to settle your case without filing a lawsuit. It's faster, and you can also save money. For instance, you won't have the expense of preparing for trial, and you won't have to pay your lawyer as much if you settle without a trial. Most lawyers charge less when they settle presuit than they charge to take a case to trial. In Florida, for example, an attorney gets a third of your settlement if you reach a presuit agreement with the insurance company. If that case is put into the court system, the attorney fee increases to 40 percent of the settlement. That means you save thousands of dollars by not going to court.

PAYING FOR YOUR CASE

Sometimes, though, it pays to invest in a case. I had a client recently who was rear-ended and suffered a back injury. That kind of case is typically worth around $50,000, but this client was wealthier than most people and had a high-quality life that was severely restricted as a result of this accident.

To drive home how badly she'd been hurt, we spent $6,000 to make a day-in-the-life video showing how compromised she was by her injuries. It's a documentary. We started filming the first thing in the morning to show how hard it was for her to just get out of bed. She needed help getting dressed. We showed how hard it was for her to simply run errands. We had a series of interviews with her family and friends, and we documented the great work she'd done in her community. It was very persuasive in showing how this great woman's life had been severely compromised, and I sent it to the adjuster. I wanted the adjuster to know, like, and trust our client and want to give her fair compensation for her injuries.

The adjuster knew we had a reputation for filing lawsuits, and she could see that we were willing to invest in this case to prove how badly our client was hurt. In the end, we were able to get our client three times what she normally would have made on a case like this.

When looking for an attorney to represent you, ask how they handle the costs of trial preparation, such as hiring expert witnesses or conducting certain studies to help prove your damages.

Different lawyers handle these expenses differently, and

there are different methodologies coming out now that are changing the rules on how to deal with the big expenses up front.

There are companies that will finance these expenses, but they either do so at a high interest rate or they do it on a contingency that allows them to get repaid from the settlement or verdict. The interest rate on a loan can be 10 percent to 12 percent. But the contingency fee interest is absurdly high, like 24 percent. However, with a contingency, if you lose your case, you repay nothing. But if you win, the lender gets a walloping chunk of your settlement.

The key to using "contingency fee funding" for any reason is to keep the time between when that advance of funds made and the time when you get a settlement paid as short as possible. Time at a high interest rate is what makes these contingency funding deals dangerous. The key to using them wisely is to use the money for only a short period of time. The longer your case drags on, the more you'll pay in interest, and that could end up gnawing a giant hole in your settlement.

The best-case scenario is hiring a firm that covers most of the case costs and expenses for you. For example, our firm will use our own financing at a much lower interest rate to pay for the expenses. That way, we can keep the interest on costs very low for our clients. Our low interest on cost expenses paid for the client's case saves our clients a lot of money.

WHAT TO EXPECT FROM YOUR LAWYER

If you're looking around for a lawyer and you're drawn to that one lawyer in your area who always seems to be on billboards or advertising on television, keep in mind that that prominent lawyer is not likely to handle your case himself. They may meet with you and shake your hand, but 90 percent of those prominent lawyers will assign your case to another lawyer in their office.

That's not to say you won't get good representation. Some large personal injury firms are run like large corporations. Your case gets assigned to a team, and that team systematically develops your case according to the firm's proven practices. The firm's system ensures efficiency and reliable outcomes. They know how to make your case valuable over time.

Some of these firms even have requirements that the lawyers on staff go to trial (and win) a minimum number of times per year. One of those was attorney John Morgan. If you worked as an attorney for Morgan and you didn't take at least three cases to trial each year, he fired you. He said lawyers who weren't willing to go to trial were just shitty, settlement-mill attorneys, and he wanted nothing to do with them. He kept only his best lawyers, and it paid off for his clients. That doesn't mean that every case at his firm goes to trial, but insurance companies are cognizant of the firm's willingness to go to court, and that alone improves the plaintiff's bargaining position.

Don't expect your lawyer to negotiate his fees with you. As I mentioned, most personal injury attorneys will ask for 33 percent of your settlement if the case doesn't get put into litigation. They will ask for 40 percent if a lawsuit is filed. In most states, those percentages are dictated by the state's bar association. Injury lawyers won't charge more because they don't want to be reprimanded by the bar. At the same time, very few lawyers will be willing to take your case for a lower percentage.

There are situations involving catastrophic injury and deep-pocket defendants that demand a reduced fee. An example would be if you are involved in a "perfect trifecta" case. That's when the injury is death, paralysis, or catastrophic; the liability is clear; and the defendant is at fault and/or has committed reckless conduct. In cases like these where the defendant is a huge corporation, insurance company, or ultrawealthy person, you should ask the lawyer to reduce the fee to 25 percent if the case can be settled in the prelitigation phase. If they won't do that, I suggest walking out. Trifecta cases can be maximized with minimum effort, and the client needs to be given a fee that meets the needs of the claim. Keep in mind that it must be a perfect case. If only two aspects are there, then the fee should remain the same as any case.

Be wary of lawyers who are willing to negotiate their fees. They are usually desperate for business, which is not a sign of a successful office, or just starting out in the industry, which is not what you are looking for to maximize your injury case. Any experienced and accomplished injury lawyer won't need to reduce the fee because they will be confident in their ability to add more value into the case than the fee itself, plus they know they are simply too busy to take a case for less. Most importantly, any client who demands a fee discount on a run-of-the-mill injury case is a problem client, and that client will make the lawyer's life miserable. We routinely let people take their case to other lawyers if they demand a fee reduction.

Sometimes after an accident, the injured person has several attorneys fighting to sign the case. In those instances, the plaintiff might be tempted to find the best deal they can make with an attorney. This is a bad strategy. There is a wide gap between a legal office that can really maximize your case and a mid-level law firm that handles injury cases as well as other things. The difference in end results can be significant. We took over a case where the original attorney had negotiated a $3,000 offer from the insurance company. When we added our value to the case, it was settled for the policy limits of $100,000.

It's never been my belief that you maximize the value of a case by reducing the expenses. You don't make money cutting expenses; you make money being aggressive and pushing your business interest to its maximum value. We've never had a client tell us to cut the expenses. I can't imagine a client saying, "I want you to hire only two experts and not three. I think we can prove my case without the other expert." That would be an absurd situation, and frankly, I wouldn't tolerate such a client. I would explain that the case needs to be prosecuted, and to properly prosecute the case, we need certain experts and information. If this is a good strategy, then why would a client want to skimp on getting a cheap attorney instead of the best attorney they can afford.

THE TIMETABLE FOR YOUR CASE

At my firm, when we sign a contract with a client, we meet with them within a week or two of their accident and not more than fourteen days after their sign-up date. If there isn't a pandemic, the client will come into one of our offices and meet their legal team. We'll discuss the case, formulate a game plan, and set reasonable expectations on the case. We want our clients to know what is expected of them and what we will do over the next few months.

Over the next five months, we check in regularly with the client. We ask about their medical condition and make sure they are seeing the right people. We collect the documentation needed to prosecute their case. We will also recommend doctors and specialists for treating their conditions, as well as diagnostic testing facilities and experts to add value to the claim. We have a deep knowledge of the body, and we have an orthopedic surgeon who confers with us daily on individual claim-management issues.

People often ask why it takes so long to file a demand with the insurance company to settle a case. The truth is that it doesn't need to take that long. Many things affect the time frame necessary to properly settle an injury case. You must pay attention to a lot of different aspects of the case and make a strategic decision on how you want to maximize the claim. It is like playing chess. If you move your rook, then it causes you to run a set strategy to win. But if you attack with your bishop, it creates an entirely different future for the game. Injury cases are the same.

The factors include the insurance companies involved, including the plaintiff's, the defendant's, and any excess carriers. Some companies have a reputation for not settling, and others have reputations for being relatively fair. Other factors include the amount of each insurance policy available, past and future medical treatment, lost wages, and total economic damages, and the photographs of the property damage. If you were on a jury being asked for a $1 million settlement and the photos showed almost no property damage, would you be comfortable awarding $1 million? See how that works?

All these factors come into play, but one of the most significant ones is total care and permanent damages. According to the American Medical Association's *Guide to Permanent Impairments*, the plaintiff will need to have six months of continued subjective pain to prove a permanent soft tissue injury worthy of a doctor giving you a permanent impairment rating. That means many cases will need at least six months of continued pain and treatment to be considered a permanent injury. In Florida, New York, New Jersey, and other no-fault states, you can't get pain and suffering damages without permanent impairment. So it is necessary to wait at least six months to convince the adjuster that the soft tissue damages are permanent.

We meet again between the five- and six-month mark. This is usually right as the medical treatment is finalized. The purpose here is to review the totality of the claim and understand the value of the case. The value includes the past and future medical costs, the past and future economic and lost wage damages, and the past and future noneconomic damages, also called human damages, which include pain, suffering, disfigurement, and mental anguish. We work up a demand amount so the defendant knows how much we want to settle the case.

Over the next sixty to eighty days, we'll learn where the adjuster is going to land on their negotiated process, and we'll determine if the insurance company is going to give us a maximum reasonable value without going to suit. If the adjuster's offer is a good one, we'll accept it. If it's less than what we think the case is worth, we'll break down how much our client can get as a reasonable award through a lawsuit, how much that award might cost us to get, the time value of a reasonable award, and what the risk of going to trial might be. This allows the client an opportunity to compare the two numbers—the adjuster's presuit offer and the anticipated outcome of a lawsuit—and make a decision on how to proceed.

I'm very up front about the risk factors. That's because people usually know when there are issues in their case, but many pretend those issues aren't there or are easily explained away. For example, if a client seeking compensation for a neck injury had a preexisting neck injury, we would point out the risk of taking the case to trial. The insurance company will try to convince the jury that this accident didn't cause the injury but that the injury was already there. The client is likely to have several reasons why a jury should disregard that previous injury, but as his lawyer, I'm obligated to point out that his medical history could reduce his award (or eliminate it altogether) at trial.

You should expect to know within a year whether you will

have to go to trial. In an average case that doesn't go to trial, your attorney should be able to settle the case in three to eight months. That will vary depending on the circumstance, of course, but if you have a good attorney in a fast-moving law firm that doesn't waste time, your case should be settled within a year. If your case goes to court, the time frame will depend on which court you file in. For instance, if I file a lawsuit in Palm Beach County, I can usually get a trial date inside of eighteen months. But in Broward County, it takes about thirty months to get to a trial.

Keep in mind, too, that in some states like Florida, a judge won't let you go to trial without first attempting mediation. About 60 percent to 80 percent of all cases get settled this way. Both sides are confronted by a smart mediator who's handled a lot of cases, and this usually can get both sides to a point where they are mutually unhappy enough to agree to a settlement. The adjuster may not want to go over $300,000, you won't come down from $500,000, but if the two sides can get to $350,000 to $400,000, everybody goes home slightly dissatisfied. The case goes away, the risk goes away, and everyone has to admit that it was a good process.

EXPECT HONESTY

You need to be honest with yourself about your case. You

really need your attorney to be honest with you about your chances of winning in court. I've had to look a few clients in the eye and tell them, "Look, you're a very difficult person to get along with. We've had to bend over backward to make this easy for you and to get your case to this point. You tend to be prickly. If you get on the stand and the defense attorney pushes the right buttons, you are not going to fare well to a jury, and that jury is going to give you a verdict of zero." This is hard for most lawyers to say, but I think you need to be honest with your client. He might be better off taking the presuit settlement rather than risk angering a jury.

There are a lot of clients who see a billboard with big numbers and develop unrealistic, pie-in-the-sky expectations. A lot of people think they have a million-dollar case, but very few do. However, if there is a slim chance of a million-dollar verdict and the client wants to swing for the fence, we go for it. I love swinging for the fences. I don't worry too much about losing my shirt in those cases—I can usually get enough to cover our expenses, get a fee, and put some money in my client's pocket—but it is vital that the client understand the risks involved. Juries are unreliable.

Clients also need to understand that the attorney they hired may be working on their case even when they are not in close contact with them. As a client, you have to take a leap of faith and realize that your lawyer is working in the background, talking to your doctors and adjustor, collecting documents, and filing paperwork.

One thing lawyers can't do is pay your debts off in anticipation of a settlement. In many states, including Florida, the bar association has declared it unethical for lawyers to pay their clients' debts. We can help them find doctors who will not harass them about an overdue bill, and we can make sure the client's MedPay and PIP accounts are being properly used to pay for medical expenses. We try to maximize every avenue available to us to keep bills low.

Still, bills are likely to mount in many cases because the client is out of work at the same time that they are facing staggering medical expenses. So one thing we can do for our clients is to contact the billing companies and ask them to send us the bills so that we can pay them from the settlement when the funds become available. We can ask doctors to sign a letter of protection and accept a lien on the case so they can be paid when it settles.

Another option for clients is to use nonrecourse financing, which is a type of commercial loan where the funder is repaid from the proceeds of your settlement. The lender can't go after your other assets, and if you lose the case, you pay nothing. However, these types of advances carry a high interest rate and have to be repaid in full when your case settles. This type of loan doesn't require a credit check, and you don't even need to be employed. Your credit score and credit history are irrelevant. The only thing that matters is the strength of your case.

THE VALUE AN ATTORNEY BRINGS

If your case is large enough or complicated enough, there are a couple of reasons why you'd want to hire a personal injury attorney to represent you.

First of all, an excellent lawyer with a lot of experience is almost a doctor in this case. They haven't gone to medical school necessarily, but they understand how the body works and the ramifications of your injuries. Personal injury lawyers learn a lot about medicine, particularly about the type of injuries we commonly see in auto accidents. A good attorney will understand your physiology and what's going on in your body. They know what's wrong with you, and they know how to sell it. They know how to describe it to an adjuster. They know what it can lead to. They can get doctors and move them down the path of treating your injury effectively.

For example, I had a client who was injured in an auto accident. His shoulder was killing him, but the doctors couldn't figure out what the problem was. He went to an orthopedist, and the orthopedist couldn't find the problem, so the orthopedist sent my client to a shoulder expert. The shoulder guy couldn't find anything but a mild fusion in the guy's shoulder. That problem couldn't cause as much pain as my client was reporting, so the shoulder guy concluded my client was "a bit of a baby."

But I had a theory. I called a friend of mine who is a spinal surgeon and told him that I thought my client was experiencing what's called referred pain. The problem, I surmised, was not in his shoulder but in his neck. I thought he had a herniated disk in his neck that was shooting pain to his shoulder. The spine expert agreed to see my client, and lo and behold, he found a herniated disk. My client had an operation on his neck, and his shoulder pain disappeared. What's more, he picked up a $100,000 settlement.

I've had that experience a gazillion times. Specialists are so focused on one area of the body that they don't take into account problems elsewhere. That's when you need a lawyer with experience in medical cases. After thirty years in this business, I can read an MRI as well as a doctor.

This kind of experience and knowledge helps attorneys get the most out of their client's injury. That's why if the adjuster offers you $300,000, I can get you $1 million. If the adjuster offers you $10,000, I can get you a $45,000 offer. It's statistically proven that lawyers add value to your case, and in my practice, I know I add value.

I've had many clients come to me and say, "I've been

offered this much to settle my case. Can you do better?"
And in many cases, I've told them that I can and will do
better and that if I don't, I'll cut my fee. You will pocket at
least what they've already offered you.

And I've never lost in that proposition.

CHAPTER SEVEN

CASES THAT ABSOLUTELY NEED A LAWYER

Although this book has given you all the tools you need to negotiate your own settlement with an insurance company after an auto accident, there are certain personal injury cases that you should never try to settle without a good lawyer at your side. These are the kind of cases that are so complex that you need expert help to ensure your rights aren't compromised. These cases include medical malpractice, sexual harassment, mass torts, product liability, medical product defects, nursing home abuse and neglect, and a few others.

MEDICAL MALPRACTICE

It's human nature to try to simplify things. We like simplicity. We tend to think in terms of good guys and bad guys. We also like to think in terms of simple cause and effect. So when we read a story about how three hundred people took hydroxychloroquine and were cured of COVID-19, we quickly reach the conclusion that hydroxychloroquine is the answer to the coronavirus pandemic.

But then the scientists step up and say, "Hold on a minute. We need to test this conclusion."

So they do a scientific study that shows the sample size of three hundred people is not large enough to reach that conclusion. When they do double-blind studies with hydroxychloroquine and placebos, they find that the drug doesn't make any difference at all. In fact, they learn that hydroxychloroquine can cause serious heart rhythm problems, blood and lymph system disorders, kidney injuries, and liver problems. The situation, we learn, is not so black and white. Yet people will still insist on reaching a simple conclusion: Joe Smith took hydroxychloroquine and got better. I'm going to take hydroxychloroquine, too. They refuse to think in terms of complexity. They hate the idea of complex systems with an infinite number of variables that could lead to an untold number of outcomes. They just want to believe in simple cause and effect.

It's rarely that simple. Say you went to the hospital for a knee operation. You have a successful surgery, but when you wake up, your arm is in great pain. What's going on here? I came in for my knee, and now my arm is hurting? The doctor must have screwed up somehow!

Well, the truth is—and what science will tell you—is that when people are put under anesthesia, about 1 percent will throw a blood clot. Blood clots can cause muscle or nerve damage in peripheral parts of your body. They can go down to your heart and kill you. It's just one of the risks you face when you have surgery, and there is nothing the doctor can do to prevent it. If they give you blood thinners to prevent a clot, you face even worse consequences, such as bleeding out on the operating table. So now that you're lying in your hospital bed with a throbbing arm and numbness that will last the rest of your life, is that medical malpractice?

No. The doctor didn't do anything wrong, but many patients lying in that bed will refuse to understand the complexity of the system.

Medical malpractice cases are rarely cut and dried. To win a medical malpractice case, you have to prove that negligence occurred and that the damage you suffered was a result of that negligence. That is a significant endeavor. You simply can't prove that without a medical expert, expert testimony, and an expert understanding of how medical malpractice works in your state. Every state has complex medical negligence laws. States often go out of their way to protect doctors. Overcoming these legal and scientific hurdles is impossible for a layman.

In medical malpractice cases, not only do you have to know what you're doing, but you also have to do it quickly. Most states have limited the amount of time you have to bring a medical malpractice case to court. Out of all the types of cases we handle in our office, medical malpractice is the most complex and the most dangerous to handle. Even the presuit requirements are difficult to meet. In Florida, for instance, there's an entire statute describing the steps you must take before you can file a suit, and you have only two years to act before the statute of limitations runs out. Even before you can file a suit, you have to find a doctor to give you an affidavit explaining why there was negligence. You even have to offer the information to the other side and give them the opportunity to take your statement and take discovery before you can sue. In fact, you have to engage in active, lawsuit-like behavior before you can sue, and that usually requires that you find an attorney to represent you.

This is not to say that mistakes don't happen in the hospital. They do. I had one client, a doctor, tell me that 80 percent of the people who go to the hospital have something negligent done to them. They are given the wrong pill or the wrong dosage. But most of the time, no harm is done. No harm, no foul. A nurse notices the wrong medication was administered and treats the patient with a counteracting drug. On other occasions, there is no serious harm or lasting damage caused by the negligence.

You can still take action in those cases, but it won't be a malpractice lawsuit. When my wife went in to give birth to our first child, she received an epidural to ease the pain of childbirth. But the epidural feed was put in upside down, so the anesthesia went north instead of south, and my wife's lungs became numb, and she could not feel herself breathing. She panicked because she thought she was suffocating. The nurses figured out the problem quickly and fixed it, but when I got the hospital bill, the charges for anesthesia were five times what they should have been. They had charged me for the faulty epidural, the drugs they gave Esther to get feeling back in her lungs, and the new epidural that was administered for the actual delivery. The delivery was fine, and Esther was unhurt. There wasn't any malpractice because there weren't any damages.

But there was no way I was going to pay that anesthesia bill. I called the hospital and told them why. I wasn't going to sue for medical malpractice, but I let them know that they had screwed up and needed to take responsibility for what happened. They took the anesthesia expenses off my bill.

MEDICAL PRODUCT DEFECTS

This type of case is also very complicated. And even if a medical device caused serious injury, the cost of pursuing a case is so significant that many people don't feel it's worth it.

For starters, the company that produced the product is never going to admit their product is faulty. They probably spent billions of dollars developing the product, testing it, getting it approved by the federal government, and marketing it. They're not about to say, "Sorry. Here's some money for your trouble. We will pull the product off the market." That never happens.

This is why medical product defects often end up as class-action lawsuits. In a class action, several plaintiffs sign up as a group to sue someone. An individual case worth $60,000 isn't worth enough to justify the cost of the scientific studies needed to beat one of these companies. But a group of lawyers who've signed up several clients can afford to spend the seven figures they need to prove a defective device hurt their clients. They get the benefit of all the science and all the prosecution and all the group think required to go after one of these companies.

We were involved in one case several years ago against a manufacturer who made the lead wires on implanted defibrillators. The leads were designed to give the heart a tiny shock when it went into atrial fibrillation. The problem was that the leads were misfiring and putting patients' hearts into atrial fibrillation before shocking them back out of it. One patient in Minnesota said it was like living with a ticking time bomb in your chest. I think about a dozen people died, but the devices were very difficult to fix because the surgery to remove them was risky.

There were clear product damage and clear liability in that case, but you could never get the company to give you any money unless you had a lawyer. You could make a claim; you could give them a call. But if you wanted any compensation for having this faulty product embedded in your chest, you needed to be part of a group.

In another case we're involved in against a big drugmaker, the budget for pursuing the action is $1.5 million. That is way more than one individual could afford, but we have about 10,000 people signed up, so the cost of pursuing that claim is only $550 per person, not $1.5 million. You would be foolish to pursue a case like that on your own. You wouldn't get anywhere.

A class-action lawsuit is when a group of people suffers similar or identical injuries because of an identical wrong committed by the defendant. A mass tort is when a lot of people suffered from a wrong committed by a single defendant, but everyone suffered differently. It's one company and it's one product, but there are a gazillion claims, each one asserting something slightly different. A mass tort claim is a way of efficiently handling all those actions. Every claim is handled in the same jurisdiction, and the judge impanels a group of lawyers to work out a settlement.

Once the court gets a handle on this and the parties come up with a settlement figure, they create a matrix to determine how to distribute payments to plaintiffs. In the case of a drug that injured people, those who developed cancer will get X amount whereas those who suffered kidney damage will get Y amount. Older patients who used the drug longer will get Z amount and so on. Everyone who signed on the mass torts action will fall into a box on that matrix, and that box will determine your settlement amount. You just have to figure out how to get in a box and to get a bigger box. You really need to have someone represent you.

PRODUCT LIABILITY CASES

We've already talked about medical devices, which are just one form of product liability. But nearly all product liability cases are going to require a lawyer. Even if you don't need a lawyer, a lawyer will help you get fair compensation.

Say, for example, you buy a ladder. You take it home and set it up precisely the way you're supposed to and you climb up and stand on a rung to fix an electrical wire. While you're doing the repair, a rivet breaks on the ladder rung, and you get electrocuted and fall to the ground, paralyzed for life.

It's possible that you could get a settlement from the ladder company without a lawyer simply by calling them up. They may even give you an impressive settlement, like $1 million.

The problem is, how do you know how to value your case so that you can get a top-value settlement? They offered you $1 million, but what if your case is worth $10 million? Internally, the ladder company might be thinking, Let's pay this guy quick. If he gets a lawyer, they may find out that we've had thousands of ladders losing rivets. We don't want that. So even when you pay a lawyer 30 percent or 40 percent, it could result in you getting a lot more money in the long run.

Regardless, you'll still need to prove your case. Most companies will not roll over and admit their product failed. They'll say it was user error. They'll say the ladder was old or wasn't maintained properly. They'll say there was a problem in the supply chain that caused the rung to break. In serious cases, the defendants will throw up a wall of subterfuge, and you'll need an attorney to break through it.

SEXUAL HARASSMENT

Although we're in the Me Too era, it's not easy to win a

sexual harassment claim these days without a lawyer. The statute of limitations is short, and there is a complicated statutory scheme you have to follow when pursuing a case like this.

The first thing you must do is file a complaint with the Equal Employment Opportunity Commission (EEOC). You have to do this before you can file a lawsuit. The EEOC has a certain amount of time in which to investigate your claim, and then they issue a conclusion of no action or a right-to-sue letter, which allows you to file suit against the person in the business whom you feel made unwanted sexual advances. You can get a lawyer before going to the EEOC, but you can't sue anyone until the EEOC says you can.

Most people don't know this, but sexual harassment could be anybody on anybody. Usually, it's a man on a woman, but it can also be man on man, woman on man, or some other combination. And what might be considered sexual harassment from one person might be welcomed attention from someone else. I worked several years ago with a lawyer who was very fat and very flirtatious with the women in the office. We also worked with a good-looking, former baseball player who would say the same type of things to women in the office. But it was the fat guy who got sued for sexual harassment, not the young stud.

Often, sexual harassment actions can morph into something much larger. An example might be if a woman working at a company is being harassed by someone in middle management. She complains to upper management about the guy and winds up getting fired herself. So now you have a whistleblower wrongful termination action on top of the sexual harassment action.

People also frequently confuse the terms *assault* and *battery*. Sexual assault is verbal, and sexual battery is physical. Assault is saying unconditionally that you're coming to hurt someone and causing them to be in fear. So if you say, "I'm coming over in fifteen minutes to kick your ass," that's assault. But if you say, "If you don't give me the car keys, I'll come over there and kick your ass," that's not assault. Harassment is creating unreasonable fear with inappropriate behavior. Sexual assault and sexual harassment are not synonymous. You can get civil damages for sexual harassment, but it's not a criminal offense.

The point here is that you really need a lawyer to help you sort through all this. It's also true that people who have been taken advantage of at this level cannot advocate for themselves. There is too much sexual tension in many offices, and there are people who are going to blame the victim. The victims deserve someone to advocate for them because some people are going to say, "You're the one who was turned on to him, not him to you. You caused this. You're the one who should be sued."

These are incredibly emotional cases. The victim is often referred to as "damaged goods," which means they have a sexual history that will hurt their case. Even in the Me Too movement, women still must overcome any history of sexual activity that has any deviant behavior permitted. So if the woman has claimed she was brutalized before, that will hurt her, even though in reality this is very common. Facing your assailant is impossible to do without someone to be your knight. Plus, it is hard to sell your case having actual value. When a sex victim tries to sell their own case, they look like a prostitute.

WHISTLEBLOWER

The United States did not have a whistleblower law until Abraham Lincoln needed one during the Civil War. The federal government was being defrauded by contractors selling supplies and materiel to the Union Army. For instance, companies sold the North crates of rifles, but many of the crates came packed with sawdust instead of guns. The government was too busy waging war to investigate these cases, but if a private citizen discovered fraud and helped the government recoup its money, Lincoln would give them a portion of the recovered funds. That law eventually became codified as the False Claims Act.

Today, there are a number of laws that all relate back to that first law created during the Civil War. These laws can be used by whistleblowers to report fraud against the government, military, healthcare, or infrastructure contracts. Even the IRS has a special whistleblower law for large tax fraud situations.

If you have inside secret information that the government is getting defrauded in any way, there is likely a qui tam law that allows the government to bring legal action and sue for the return of the overpayments, as well as an award of a huge penalty. If the government decides to pursue the fraud and collects money because of your inside information, then you will be awarded about 15 percent of those funds. If the government does not want to pursue that case, they must then give the whistleblower the opportunity to sue on behalf of the government and collect the wrongly paid funds. The Latin term *qui tam* came from an old saying: "Qui tam pro domino rege quam pro se ipso in hac parte sequitur," which means, "[He] who sues in this matter for the king, as well as for himself." The government literally gives the legal action back to the whistleblower, and that person is permitted to pursue the fraud using their own private attorney. If the whistleblower brings the lawsuit and then wins any funds for Uncle Sam, the whistleblower is entitled to keep between 15 percent and 30 percent of what is recovered. The exact percentage of the whistleblower's award will be set by the judge. It will depend on how much work the whistleblower put into the case. There are a number of whistleblower laws that also provide job protection to whistleblowers because of the personal and professional risks they take reporting fraud and sometimes pursuing that fraud.

To start a qui tam case, the whistleblower must have inside information that is not known to the public and has not already been disclosed to the government. When there are two or more whistleblowers, the first to file gets paid. The whistleblower first creates a position paper that details the fraud. They then must submit that position paper to a special division of the attorney general's office for review. The government then decides whether to proceed with the case. If they like the case, they will interview the whistleblower and investigate the matter and then take action using the US Attorney's Office. If they do not like it or feel the information isn't enough to bring a lawsuit, they turn the information back to the whistleblower, who can then bring their own action against the defrauding agency.

Many qui tam whistleblower cases allege fraud against the government in the healthcare industry. The government spends hundreds of billions annually on drugs, hospital care, outpatient services, and nursing home care through Medicare, Medicaid, and other government healthcare programs. The government demands all healthcare providers submit accurate reimbursement requests that comply with the billing laws related to any government payer of those healthcare bills. Many medical doctors, hospital systems, and drug companies do not follow the rules. They bill the government for services they never provided, for unnecessary services, or for unnecessary and expensive procedures.

Other qui tam lawsuits are filed through the IRS, and others result from shady practices in defense contracts, securities and commodities, and pharmaceuticals. One of the biggest cases involved a drug maker, which was ripping off the government on the drugs it was selling. The company had to pay $3 billion back to the federal government in ripped-off funds.

One case we brought involved the manufacturer of helicopter parts for military aircraft. The company was saving money by using outdated and degraded chemicals in the production of the onboard keyboards for a well-known military helicopter. This could pose a dangerous problem for the operators if the keyboard cracked in a warzone during a battle. A woman who worked for the company reported what was going on, and the government sued. The company was found at fault and had to pay over $50 million back to the government and replace all the products they'd made with outdated chemicals.

These cases can result in huge settlements for both the government and the whistleblower. The problem is that the system the government uses for this process is secretive and one-sided. The government won't keep you in the loop.

Often, the whistleblower finds out he didn't solidify his place in line for his portion of the recovered money. Many times, the whistleblower will deliver a position paper that is insufficient, and then a later whistleblower provides the operative information that leads to a huge repayment. In that case, the second whistleblower gets the money! Lots of people have taken cases to the government under this law and have never been paid.

How do you ensure you keep your place in line? How do you create a position paper that works? How do you report large corporate tax fraud to the IRS so that you can be granted a part of the money the IRS recovers? You need a lawyer. You need a lawyer to write your position paper. You need a lawyer to sit in your meeting with the Justice Department and document your position and the information you provide. You need a lawyer who previously worked for the government and knows what the government needs to bring the fraud action. Then, at the end of the case, when the government goes from being your friend to not wanting to pay you a fair share of the recovery, your lawyer is there to protect your money. Splitting your share with a lawyer helps ensure you get paid at all.

NURSING HOME NEGLIGENCE

These are very similar to medical malpractice cases. The hardest part about a case like this is the fact that the people who are being abused are not likely to live much longer. Defendants use this to undermine the value of any claim. You can make a claim after a relative of yours was abused, and you might get some money. But the corporations who operate these facilities are not likely to roll over so easily.

Say you have a relative who develops a pressure sore on their heel. The sore gets gangrenous, and your relative's foot has to be amputated. You might be able to handle that claim by yourself, but you'll never get full value if you don't hire a lawyer. A lawyer will develop the expert testimony that reveals that the gangrene resulted from negligence and was completely avoidable. Even if your relative is close to the end of their life, you and your relative deserve to be compensated for that negligence, and an attorney would help you get it.

AUTO ACCIDENTS INVOLVING COMMERCIAL CARRIERS

These kinds of settlements demand the expertise of a lawyer, too.

Commercial drivers carry a strict level of responsibility that goes beyond what's required of noncommercial drivers, so there are many things a lawyer familiar with those rules can do to develop evidence and create liability.

It's often not easy to pin that liability on a commercial driver, but it helps to know the federal rules and regulations that govern commercial drivers. The standards for someone driving an eighteen-wheeler are strict and more extensive than they are for people driving a car. To win against commercial carriers, you have to know what those standards are. If you have an expert attorney, you can significantly increase the value of your case because commercial carriers are required to carry large insurance policies.

About four years ago, I was involved in a case involving the driver of a Toyota Camry that was merging onto the highway and was literally crushed by an eighteen-wheeler. The Toyota driver was in a coma for five or six months, and when he came out of it and read the police report, it indicated that he was at fault in the accident. He had merged right into the underbelly of the truck.

Still, with over a million dollars in medical bills, he called the trucking company and asked for help. They declined to settle with him. You were at fault, they said, and we can't pay you for that. The Toyota driver called an attorney and got a similar response. Sorry, the lawyer said, you can't turn left under a truck.

I got involved about eight months after the accident. I met the Toyota driver in the hospital and got a copy of the accident report. When I investigated the case, I found out that the truck had a video camera that had been running at the time of the accident. The footage, I learned, revealed that the truck driver had been merging right at the same time that my client had been merging left. Neither driver had been aware of the other. So my client wasn't, in fact, 100 percent at fault. He was only 50 percent at fault. What's more, the truck's black box backed this up.

We eventually got a seven-figure settlement for this poor guy lying in a hospital bed. But the only way we were able to do that was by being familiar with interstate trucking laws, knowing that the truck may have been recording and had a black box, and realizing that there were other reports that had to be filed by the trucking company that would support our claim. Our client would never have gotten a settlement without us.

BOAT AND CRUISE ACCIDENT CASES

We've already talked about these cases earlier in the book, but it bears repeating that boat and cruise accident cases should not be handled by anyone without a lawyer.

For one thing, the statute of limitations on cruise cases are exceptionally short and harsh. The injury must be noticed to the cruise company within six months of the date of onset, and any lawsuit must be filed within a year of the injury. This is an unbreakable rule, and the cruise company knows this deadline and uses it to its advantage. I was once asked by a cruise adjuster to "wait till after Christmas to discuss a settlement" only to realize my client went on a Christmas cruise, and on December 27, the case would be beyond the statute of limitations!

So my advice is to be wary of these cases. They are hard to prove, and the cruise company will almost never settle without going to court. That's okay, though, because there are many law firms (including mine) that handle cruise boat cases. If you've been hurt on a cruise boat, find one of these lawyers to represent you.

As for boating cases, these are also often complex, and the average boater doesn't have the experience or knowledge to handle them without an attorney. The injuries in these cases are usually serious, and the claim is usually against the captain of the ship. There are crew issues, product manufacturing problems, and far too many obscure boating rules and regulations for a normal boater to know. You won't get a fair settlement by going it alone on one of these cases.

As you can see, some personal injury cases are often complicated and require expert representation. The stakes for many of these cases are also higher, and that's another sign that you may need to hire a lawyer to represent you.

If you find yourself involved in one of these cases—or any

complicated or serious motor vehicle accident in which the damages are significant—it never hurts to call an attorney and explain your circumstances. If they think they have the expertise and can drive value into your case, they'll let you know, and you can take steps to hire them.

CONCLUSION

Motor vehicle accidents can happen in a split second but can take years to untangle. When you're injured in an accident that wasn't your fault, it can feel like a monumental task to get the compensation you deserve for your injuries, property damage, and pain and suffering. The other side tries to minimize your condition or suggest that it's been exaggerated or invented. Insurance adjusters drag their feet, discredit the value of your claims, and use subtle negotiating tricks to get your claim settled for as little as possible. They negotiate every day, all day long and are experts. You, on the other hand, may have never been in a serious auto accident before, and the process of settling your case is confusing and fraught with uncertainty. What if I miss a deadline? What if my headache is actually brain damage?

First, you need to be prepared before anything happens.

You can do this by keeping a copy of this checklist in your glove box. This form is also downloadable at www.notagoodneighbor.com.

POST-ACCIDENT CHECKLIST

Stay calm. Safety is the first priority. Make sure you are not badly injured. Then call the police.

Make sure you always have your driver's license on you when you are driving.

Keep a copy of your automobile insurance in the car. That way, it is always easy to get to when you are in your car.

I keep my registration in the glove box, too. Some people say not to do that, but I do it.

It never hurts to have a small first-aid kit and an emergency kit in your trunk. The emergency kit can even include a few orange cones or flags to keep you safe if you break down and must pull off the road.

If you are involved in an accident, first make sure you are okay. Take a moment after the accident. You do not need to jump out of the car. The smoke in the car is from the airbags. Cars do not explode like in the movies after an accident. You can take a moment before jumping out of the car. Remember, your body will NOT hurt right after the accident. Your adrenaline is pumping, and it causes the pain to dissipate. Once you are sure you are not too hurt, you can get this checklist out of the glove box. You will need it. It is almost impossible to think clearly after an accident. You will need a list of steps to follow so you protect your rights directly after an accident.

- First, do NOT leave. Do not pull away. Stay at the scene.
- After you make sure you are okay, make sure the other party is okay. Most of the time, the wreck was caused by a mistake, and the other party will feel terrible about causing the accident. If you check on them, you can show you are a good person and also talk to them and see if they apologize. That apology can help you out in the future.
- Call 911 and get the police and an ambulance to come. Anyone in need of help must get medical attention as soon as possible. Even if the injuries are minor, call the police. The police create a record of the property damage, the fault, and even note the injuries. If no one is injured, it will be tempting to avoid calling the police. Some at-fault drivers will even ask for "a break. Don't be swayed. Call the police and make a report. There are too many stories about nice people who were injured, but because they did not call the police and document the fault, their claim for damages was undermined when the at-fault driver changes his story and doesn't admit fault.

- In many jurisdictions, it is possible to file a police report after you leave the scene. But that is not an effective way to document your case. Get the police report filed up front by calling the police immediately.
- If you can, take photographs of the vehicles right after the accident in the positions they are in. That is the best evidence you can obtain. Once you get the scene photos with the cars, you should try to move your car out of traffic to the side of the road and turn on your hazard lights.
- Take more photos of the damage to the cars and the surrounding area. Pay attention to the lighting sequence if the accident happened at an intersection controlled by lights.
- Keep a small notebook in the glove box and take notes. Get witness names, addresses, emails, and cell phone numbers, and make sure you know their story. Look for cameras on the adjacent properties. Write down the details of the accident scene to preserve as much evidence as you can. Take down the defendant's driver's information and make sure you or the police get his name, address, cell phone number, and email address.
- Don't be shy. Talk to any witnesses. They will want to talk to you if you are not at fault.
- If an insurance person comes to the scene, do not sign any papers. You can sign the accident report information for the police, but make sure it is accurate first.
- Do NOT admit fault. If you are at fault, do not discuss

the incident with anyone at the scene. Do not give your driver's license to anyone but the police officer to review.

- You may not leave the accident scene until after the police tell you it is safe to leave.

STARTING YOUR CLAIM

After the accident, you need to start the claim process. You can do this by calling your insurance company. Ask them to open a new claim. Explain the facts of what happened at the wreck. Be clear in your story about what happened. Don't meander between the facts and any feelings or any injury you suffered. Give the adjuster the facts. Be precise. Be clear. When asked, you must describe your injury in general terms from head to toe. Make a list of all your injuries—literally anything that is bothering you. If your tooth is hurting after an accident, tell the adjuster. If your old back injury flared up, tell the adjuster.

Here are some other key steps to remember:

- Call the police department and find out when the accident report will be ready for you to pick up. Make sure you get a copy of the accident reports as filed by the police.
- Keep detailed notes on all your conversations. Write down the date, whom you spoke to from your insurance company, and the substance of the conversation. Write

down all your injuries in an injury log. Track your medical treatment by putting down the doctor, the date, the prognosis, and the treatment you are getting.

· Call the automobile repair shop to get an estimate on the property damage.

· If you are asked to provide a statement to either insurance company, you will need to make a hard call: either you are going to go this alone, or you are going to need to hire a personal injury lawyer to help you through the interview.

It can all feel daunting. But that's why I wrote this book.

This book is intended to be a guide to help you find your way through the thicket of issues that rises in the aftermath of a motor vehicle accident. My goal has been to give you the information you need to decide whether to hire an attorney to maximize the value of your case. I think many of you will decide after reading this that you don't need an attorney, but others, I'm sure, will decide that an attorney makes a lot of sense.

Either way, my hope is that you'll use this book to save you time and money and to avoid the pitfalls that are inherent in these cases.

I also hope it gives you some peace of mind. Even if you wind up hiring an attorney to help you get a settlement, this book will help you better understand the process and be in a position to help your attorney get full value out of your case.

Keep in mind that the insurance companies are primarily interested in one thing and one thing only: helping you as little as possible. Insurance companies are insanely profitable because they get you to buy more insurance than you need and then pay you as little as possible when you make a claim. The insurance company—whether it's the other driver's insurance or your own—is not fighting for you. They are fighting for their own profits.

Use this book as your weapon as you fight for yourself. Use it to determine if your case is simple enough for you to handle on your own. Or conversely, use it to decide that you need to hire an expert. Most of us only rarely, if ever, are injured in auto accidents, so keep this book as a reference for when you need it.

The key thing to remember is that you are the best person to protect your interests. Your insurance company won't. The police officer who arrives on the scene of your accident won't. The other driver certainly won't.

You have to rely on yourself.

GETTING THE RIGHT INSURANCE

Your preparation for an accident starts long before you get behind the wheel. It starts by carrying the insurance policy that is right for you. Not only will you need to understand your state's insurance requirements, but you also need to ensure that your liability coverage is large enough to protect you when you're at fault in an accident. You also want to make sure you have sufficient medical coverage and that you're covered if the at-fault driver is not carrying insurance or is not carrying enough insurance.

When driving, understand where the danger spots are, and use extra caution. There are over seven million auto accidents in the United States every year, and about a third of those accidents result in injuries.

The most common automobile accident is a rear-end collision, so avoid driving too close to the car in front of you. If someone is tailgating you, move to the right and let that aggressive driver pass. Always use your turn signals. Be particularly cautious in big intersections; about a quarter of all serious crashes result from T-bone collisions and sideswipes. These happen when you're making a left-hand turn, and your view of oncoming traffic may be obscured by a facing vehicle. At busy intersections, where pedestrians may be in crosswalks or cyclists might be taking up part of a lane, take the time to sort out the best way to proceed. Don't rush through and hope for the best.

By the same token, avoid racing to beat a red light. Don't make rolling turns on a red light. Check all your blind spots before changing lanes.

Head-on collisions occur when the front of a car strikes a telephone pole, a tree, or another vehicle, and most of these are caused by distracted driving, drowsiness, or slippery roads. So let me join the chorus chanting this ubiquitous warning: Don't text and drive. When you glance down at your phone looking for just the right emoji, your car can travel the distance of a football field.

BEFORE LEAVING THE SCENE

Still, accidents happen.

When they do, use the confidence you've gained from this book to react with a cool head at the accident scene, taking pictures, shooting video, interviewing witnesses, and asserting your innocence to the police officer on the scene.

When you've been hurt, it's crucial that you get immediate medical treatment. Go to the hospital for initial treatment and then seek out specialists to help with specific injuries. Do not play the hero. Remember, your injuries may not become apparent right away, and some serious medical problems may not surface for a couple of weeks. Don't assume you're fine and that you can just "walk it off."

It helps to find doctors who are sensitive to the challenges facing auto accident victims. Chiropractors, for instance, are often skilled at documenting injuries caused by trauma. They will help you get the diagnostic tests you need and whatever specialized care is called for. Chiropractors, orthopedists, and neurologists may be crucial to helping you document your injuries and build your claim. Just be aware that some doctors won't be empathetic; they are "defense doctors" who are likely to understate the seriousness of your injuries. Look for a sympathetic doctor who will get you the treatment you need and document it properly for your claim.

DO YOU NEED A LAWYER?

If, after an accident, you're not sure whether to get a lawyer, it might help if you ask yourself a series of questions. Here are the key ones:

- How serious is my injury? If your injuries are significant, it will lead to significant damages, and you will never get enough money without a lawyer. The only injuries you can handle on your own are lower-level, nonpermanent injuries.
- Was my injury caused by someone else? If you are hurt, the only way to make a claim is if you can prove someone was at fault. Sometimes that's easy to prove, such as when you're in a collision and the other driver gets

a ticket for causing it. Other times, it's not so easy to prove fault, and you might need a lawyer to help you do that.

· Does the person who injured me have the capacity to pay me for the damage I suffered? If so, how am I going to make them pay? The at-fault driver's insurance company adjuster will know the policy limits for their client, and it will become apparent whether the insurer will cover your claim. If you are going it alone, you'll have to negotiate with that adjuster. If they refuse to meet what you consider to be your lowest possible offer, you may have to hire a lawyer and file a lawsuit to get just compensation.

· If they don't have the capacity to pay, have I got enough insurance to cover myself? In this scenario, you'll likely use your own uninsured or underinsured motorist policy to compensate you for your injuries. Your insurance company can then go after the other party for reimbursement.

· If the at-fault driver can't pay and I don't have sufficient coverage, is there a third party that is the cause that I haven't thought of before? We had a case recently where a van driver was pulling into an assisted living facility in Miami. As the driver started across the sidewalk, a fourteen-year-old skateboarder appeared on the sidewalk, and the driver struck and killed him. This was a serious accident, but the van driver's insurance amounted to only $50,000. However, when we investigated, we found that the reason the boy seemed to appear out of nowhere was that he'd been hidden by an overgrown hedge along the sidewalk. The hedge belonged to the nursing home, and the nursing home had a million-dollar policy. The nursing home's insurance company eventually tendered that million dollars to the family of the boy who was killed.

SIGNING THE RELEASE

The most important, and the most dangerous, part of the process of settling your car accident case comes after you agree on a settlement amount and the insurance company requires you to sign a document called a release. This document is used by the insurance companies to ensure that once you sign the release, you sign away your right to sue— unless you specifically make sure that the release is limited to only those things you are getting money to release.

The key here is being able to read detailed legalese and complex sentence structure in a formal legal document. There is no way to sugarcoat this fact. I do not believe I can adequately prepare you for all contingencies that you will see in a release because every insurance company has their own legal documents.

My advice is to read the release very carefully. If you don't understand it, get advice. If the case is simple—such as when there are only two parties to the accident and the insurance of the defendant is able to cover the entire damages without needing any under- or uninsured motorist coverage—then the release is usually pretty straightforward.

But some cases are more complicated. For example, there may be more than one party, you are trying to collect on two different insurances, or you are going against two or more defendants. In these cases, the release is likely to be more complicated, and you may need advice before you sign off. It might be worth getting an attorney to read the release and advise you for a small fee. It would help give you peace of mind.

WHAT'S NEXT?

My call to action in this book is simple: If you've been in an auto accident that wasn't your fault and your injuries were minor, handle it yourself. Keep your case out of the legal system.

These cases, typically worth less than $30,000, are not worth taking to court. You may be able to find an attorney to represent you, but they likely won't be able to increase the value of your case, and their share of your settlement will only reduce your reward. Besides, there is no reason you can't push this through the system and get a fair settlement for yourself.

There are too many people in the world today who think their minor injury claim is worth $1 million, that the big shot attorney on all the billboards is going to turn their fender bender accident into an $820,000 settlement. The truth is, there will never be a significant payday for anyone who's in a minor injury case. It is simply too expensive to put a small case into the court system. It costs at least $20,000 for a lawyer to bring a car accident case to court, so 99 percent of these cases are settled without a lawsuit.

Don't fall victim to the false expectations set by a billboard showing plaintiffs proclaiming, "I got $820,000!" If that happened, that person wouldn't be smiling! Something terrible happened in the accident. Big firms churn and burn. In other words, they get small settlements quickly, take 33 percent of the small settlement money, pay off the doctors, and give their clients a few pennies on the dollar. These cases could be handled without an attorney.

Here's how I hope you'll use this book:

- To quickly figure out if you have an injury case worth pursuing.
- To know what steps to take before and after an accident to protect your rights. Regardless of whether you want to bring a claim, be prepared to protect yourself and your family.
- To understand what's in store for you if you do bring an

action. To know what you need to do without a lawyer and what to expect if you hire a lawyer.

- To understand why you should spend the money to purchase better insurance for yourself and your loved ones. When you recognize the danger and the vulnerability, it makes paying for the coverage a wise decision. Understanding the automobile insurance process and the different types of coverage will help you buy the best coverage for everyone in your car. You will be protected if you hurt someone, and you won't need to file for bankruptcy. If the other driver hits you and is at fault but underinsured, you are protected.

- To negotiate better. Understanding the process and getting a good idea of the true valuation of your injury will help you negotiate with adjusters, who are trained to negotiate and given advanced computer analysis on what the injury you suffered is worth. Maybe, even beyond your case, you will use the negotiation tactics we showed to help you negotiate with your spouse, your boss, or the car salesman. Just knowing the first offer is not the last offer helps. You don't have to take the first settlement offer.

- To get proper medical care. This is important for not only health reasons but also for documentation reasons. Insurance companies need to see proof of injury, and hospitals and doctors are an important part of that documentation. Knowing how to use your automobile insurance to pay for quality medical care is crucial to getting better and helping you measure and display the extent of your damages.

- To find an attorney that's right for you, if you do need to hire a lawyer. When you understand how to look for a good attorney—someone with the right experience and expertise for your level of a case—you are always going to win.

Finally, if you get to the point in your settlement negotiations where the adjuster is just being totally unfair, I hope you will call someone for help. Despite what you may hear about personal injury lawyers, a vast majority of us are committed to protecting people, and we have a deep distrust of insurance companies. We want you to maximize your amount of justice against that insurance company. Getting that quick outside opinion may help you settle the case on your own and get the money you deserve.

APPENDIX **A**

> **KEEP A COPY OF THIS CHECKLIST** in the glove compartment of your car, along with your vehicle registration and insurance policy information.

1. STOP

Never drive away. Under Florida law, leaving the scene of a car accident is a criminal offense. You may face misdemeanor or felony charges, depending on whether there were injuries or fatalities.

If your vehicle is impeding traffic and you can do so safely, move it to the side of the road. Set up flares and/or turn on your hazard lights.

2. CHECK FOR INJURIES

Assess your own condition and that of your passengers. Are there visible injuries? If you can safely do so, check in on the driver/passengers of the other vehicle(s) involved. Do not admit fault or take the blame for the accident. It is often a natural reaction to say, *"I'm so sorry—are you all right?"* Apologizing, even if it's not your fault, can be automatic for some. But it can be viewed by the insurance company as an admission of fault and used as a reason to limit or deny claims. Instead, just ask if the other driver is injured and get help.

3. CALL 911 OR THE NONEMERGENCY POLICE LINE

Even if the car accident is minor, stay put. You must report the accident if:

- ✔ The accident causes any property damage, even paint damage, to one or more vehicles.
- ✔ There are injuries or complaints of pain or discomfort.
- ✔ One or more vehicles had to be towed from the scene.
- ✔ There was a commercial vehicle involved.
- ✔ The accident involved a driver who appears to be under the influence of alcohol or drugs.

Technically, you do not have to call from the scene if there was no damage or very minimal damage to the vehicles, but you must report the accident within 10 days. However, it is the best practice, when you are not at fault, to call the police at the scene and have them fill out a report. Calling the police is free, and it will save you from a future dispute over fault, or who will pay for any property damage to the vehicles. Of course, if there is any real damage or injuries you must call the police immediately. The police will provide you with an accident report number; you can use this to obtain an accident report when they have concluded their investigation.

4. EXCHANGE CONTACT INFORMATION

Give the other driver the information on your proof of insurance card (name, policyholder name, vehicle information, insurance company name, agent name, agent phone number, and policy number). Do not give any personal information, such as your home address. Make sure to obtain the same information from the other driver(s).

5. DOCUMENT THE SCENE

The aftermath of a car accident can be chaotic. Always prioritize safety. If you can do so without interfering with police and traffic, take photos of:

- ✔ Each car
- ✔ Each license plate
- ✔ All vehicle damage
- ✔ Skid marks
- ✔ Location markers (e.g., street signs)
- ✔ Debris from the accident
- ✔ Damage to other property
- ✔ Look for street cameras or cameras on local houses or buildings. If in a residential neighborhood look for cameras on doorbells.

If you have a piece of paper, draw a sketch of the scene which shows the positions of the vehicles, pedestrians, witnesses, street locations, etc. It does not have to be a masterpiece, but get the key details in there.

6. SEEK MEDICAL ATTENTION

When you've been involved in a car accident, your body releases hormones like adrenaline and cortisol. It's our fight or flight response, and it is designed to help us power through stressful, frightening situations. A crash certainly applies. These hormones, though, can mask pain. This is why we often feel fine after a minor accident but wake up the next day with aches, pain, and discomfort.

Symptoms may take hours or even days to present themselves, but serious issues like internal bleeding and head, neck, or spinal injury can worsen if not treated quickly. Even if you feel all right or perhaps just a bit "banged up," seek medical attention. This is an important step, too, in receiving appropriate compensation and if you decide to pursue legal action.

7. NOTIFY YOUR INSURANCE COMPANY

You must report the accident to your insurance company; many require you to do so immediately. Check your policy and see how long you have. In any case, it's better to do this sooner rather than later. Give them the details of the car accident as clearly as you can, and do not guess or speculate. Just the facts. They will give you a claim number. Keep this for your records (more on this in a minute).

8. DO NOT AGREE TO A SETTLEMENT OFFER

Insurance companies are massive profit-generating entities. They want to minimize the amount they have to pay out, so they will often offer a low-ball settlement amount very early in the claims process. It may seem reasonable at first but wait. What if your injuries worsen? What if you require more intensive or ongoing treatment? What if it costs more to repair or replace your car? What if you are unable to return to work as soon as you expected?

That settlement can be quickly depleted, and you may have financial burdens that you're left to shoulder. It is best to consult with a car accident attorney before accepting any settlement offer.

On a related note, do not sign anything unless it is from law enforcement or your insurance agent.

9. KEEP RECORDS

Keep everything:

- Your photos of the accident scene, vehicle damage, and visible injuries
- Your sketch of the scene
- The other party's contact and insurance information
- The police report
- All medical records related to the accident
- All bills related to your treatment (e.g., medication, assistive devices, braces, etc.)
- Claim numbers
- A list of everyone you have spoken to (e.g., police, insurance agents, claims adjusters, etc.) and a short summary of your conversations
- All written correspondence from police, insurance companies, etc. related to your accident
- Receipts for expenses related to your accident (e.g., rental car, repair bills, transportation, etc.)

10. CHECK FOR MEDICAL PAYMENTS AUTO INSURANCE

If you have no fault insurance (PIP) or you have medical payments insurance (MED PAY) you must make sure your medical care is paid for using your automobile insurance, NOT your health insurance policy.

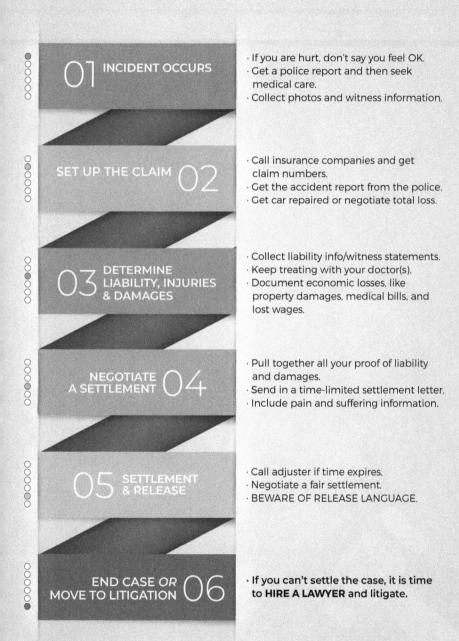

01 INCIDENT OCCURS
- If you are hurt, don't say you feel OK.
- Get a police report and then seek medical care.
- Collect photos and witness information.

SET UP THE CLAIM 02
- Call insurance companies and get claim numbers.
- Get the accident report from the police.
- Get car repaired or negotiate total loss.

03 DETERMINE LIABILITY, INJURIES & DAMAGES
- Collect liability info/witness statements.
- Keep treating with your doctor(s).
- Document economic losses, like property damages, medical bills, and lost wages.

NEGOTIATE A SETTLEMENT 04
- Pull together all your proof of liability and damages.
- Send in a time-limited settlement letter.
- Include pain and suffering information.

05 SETTLEMENT & RELEASE
- Call adjuster if time expires.
- Negotiate a fair settlement.
- BEWARE OF RELEASE LANGUAGE.

END CASE *OR* MOVE TO LITIGATION 06
- If you can't settle the case, it is time to **HIRE A LAWYER** and litigate.

APPENDIX **C** POLICE REPORT LETTER

> **SEND THIS TO THE POLICE DEPARTMENT**
> that responds to your accident. You can send it
> immediately after the accident, but understand that some
> departments may not receive the report from the officer
> for a week or two after the incident.

Date

POLICE DEPT
Address
City, State Zip

Re: ACCIDENT VICTIM NAME: *Your name*
    DATE OF ACCIDENT: *Date*

Dear SIR/MADAM:

Please accept this as my written request pursuant to the Public Record Act for information related to the following accident at your earliest convenience:

- ✔ Date of accident: *Date*
- ✔ Accident location: *Road name, City, State*
- ✔ Drivers involved: *Names of known drivers*
- ✔ Investigator: *Officer name*
- ✔ Report No.: *Number*

Please provide me with a copy of the police report, memoranda, and all investigation notes regarding the above-referenced accident.

Should there be a search fee and/or copy expenses related to this request, please notify me so I can submit payment. Please let me know if I can come to the station to pay the fee and pick up the report or if you can accept payment by phone or by check through the mail. Let me know if the report is available by electronic means.

Should you have any questions, please contact me at (XXX)XXX-XXXX.

Thank you in advance for your courtesy and cooperation.

Sincerely,

_____

Your name
Address
City, State Zip
Cell Number
Email Address

APPENDIX D INSURANCE DISCLOSURE LETTER

> **Send this to the at-fault driver's insurance company IMMEDIATELY after the accident.**

Date

INSURANCE COMPANY NAME
Address
City, State Zip

Re: Plaintiff: *Your name*
     Defendant: *Defendant's name*
     Date of Loss: *Date*
     Claim No.: *Your claim number*

Dear ADJUSTER'S NAME:

My name is FULL NAME and I was involved in the above noted accident. I would like an official disclosure of all applicable insurance limits for the above-noted person involved in this accident. If you have any written or oral statements related to this accident, please furnish them to me as well.

The Defendant caused this accident, and the accident caused me damages. I am holding the Defendant accountable for my damages and am seeking information related to insurance coverage for them, as well as my own first-party coverage to help me in this situation.

I also request that the vehicle(s) involved be preserved for examination. This request includes but is not limited to video tape(s), photographs, any physical evidence, purchase invoices, repair records, manuals, and service records involved in the incident and/or other evidence. If the vehicle is scheduled to be repaired, I instruct that all such evidence be preserved and that I am given an opportunity to examine the vehicle before it is repaired.

Please also provide a copy of all video and/or audio recordings of the accident itself as well as the area where the accident occurred for one hour before through one hour after the accident.

If you or your company is unwilling to preserve said evidence, please advise so I may make arrangements to have the evidence examined by an expert immediately.

Please be advised that your failure to produce or preserve all such evidence may result in sanctions against you and/or your insured.

I will provide any documents or records, in my possession, necessary for your investigation. You are further advised that all discussions and negotiations involving my claim(s) are to be made directly with me and only with me. I do not have representation in this incident at this time. You are only to contact or communicate with me.

Please provide me the following information, under oath, with regard to each known policy of insurance, including excess or umbrella coverage, which may provide liability insurance coverage for this claim:

1. Name of the insurer(s);

2. Name of each insured;

3. Certified copy of limits of liability coverage:

　　　a. For personal injury,

　　　b. Property damage,

　　　c. Medical expenses,

　　　d. Personal injury protection,

　　　e. Uninsured motorist and any other coverage;

4. A statement of any policy or coverage defense which your company reasonably believes is available; and

5. Certified copy of any and all policies.

The requested information must be provided within thirty (30) days from the date of this letter and must include a statement under oath by a corporate officer.

Sincerely,

_____

Your name
Address
City, State Zip
Cell Number
Email Address

APPENDIX E   **WITNESS LETTER AND QUESTIONNAIRE**

> **SEND THIS WITNESS STATEMENT to anyone you encountered at the accident scene who witnessed the collision or the behavior of any of the parties before or after the accident.**

Date

NAME
Address
City, State Zip

Dear WITNESS NAME:

My name is FULL NAME. I was involved in an accident on the above date. I was injured and I am making a claim for insurance to pay for my medical bills, lost wages, and damages.

I was told to gather witness statements. Rather than inconvenience you with a phone call or meeting, I thought this questionnaire would be easier to complete and send back to me in the enclosed stamped and pre-addressed envelope.

If you would like to speak with me, please do not hesitate to call my cell anytime (XXX)XXX-XXXX.

Thank you for any help you can offer.

Sincerely,

_____

Your name
Address
City, State Zip
Cell Number
Email Address

DATE: _____ , 20___ . _____ **WITNESS STATEMENT**

Regarding: *Your Name*
Date of accident: *Month/Day/Year*

Please fill in the following. Use the back of this page to explain any answers that can't fit on the lines.

1. Your name: _____

2. Home address: _____

3. Home phone: _____

4. Work phone: _____

5. Work address: _____

6. Name/address/phone of person who always knows how to contact you:
_____
_____

7. What, if any, is your relationship to the parties to this accident?
_____
_____

8. If one or more motor vehicles were involved in this accident, describe the vehicle(s):
_____
_____

9. If a pedestrian was involved, describe clothing and route of travel and explain involvement in the accident:
_____
_____
_____

10. If a bicycle was involved, described the bicycle and route of travel and explain involvement in the accident:
_____
_____
_____

11. What attracted your attention to the accident?
_____

12. Describe the weather and/or lighting conditions at the scene of the accident:
_____

13. Did you see the accident? ◯ Yes ◯ No

14. Did you hear the accident? ◯ Yes ◯ No

15. If so, describe where you were in relation to the accident and what you saw and heard:
_____
_____

16. If you did not see or hear the accident, did you come upon the scene after the accident had occurred? ◯ Yes ◯ No
If so, describe when you came upon the scene, what you saw, and what you heard:

_____
_____

17. If you heard any conversation, identify who said what to whom, if possible:

_____
_____
_____

18. Did you see anyone who looked injured in any way? ◯ Yes ◯ No
If so, describe your impressions:

_____
_____

19. Did you hear anyone complain of being injured? ◯ Yes ◯ No
If so, describe the party making the complaint and what was said:

_____
_____

20. Did anyone admit fault or responsibility for the accident? ◯ Yes ◯ No
If so, describe what was said:

_____
_____

21. Please give the name and address of any person who was with you or who you know to have been at the scene of the accident:

_____
_____

22. Based on what you saw and/or heard, who do you think was at fault in the accident and why?

_____
_____

23. How could this accident have been prevented?

_____
_____

24. Did you feel that drugs or alcohol played a part in this accident?
◯ Yes ◯ No
If so, explain:

_____
_____

25. Did you feel there was any hostility between the parties to the accident or that unusual conduct of any sort was involved? ◯ Yes ◯ No
If so, explain:

_____
_____

Any other impressions:

_____
_____
_____
_____
_____
_____

I have read the foregoing pages and declare under penalty of perjury that the foregoing is true and correct to the best of my knowledge.

_____
Witness Signature

SUBSCRIBED AND SWORN to before me this _____ day of _____.

_____
Notary Public

My commission expires: _____

It is best practice to get a WITNESS STATEMENT NOTARIZED. However, it is permissible to use a witness statement for settlement purposes without a notary.

APPENDIX F   MEDICARE/HEALTH INSURANCE SUBROGATION LETTER

> **THIS IS THE LETTER USED TO PUT GOVERNMENT PAYERS ON NOTICE.** If you have any connection to Medicare, you must put them on notice of your accident. This is especially true if Medicare is your primary health insurance. If you get health insurance from your employer, then it may be subject to a federal law called ERISA. This letter can also be used to put the ERISA carrier on notice as well.

Date

ATTN: SUBROGATION DEPT.
Medicare Health Insurance
PO Box 1270
Lawrence, KS 66044

Re: Insured: *Your Name*
    Date of birth: *Your Date of Birth*
    Date of accident: *Date*
    ID number: *Number*
    Photo of my Medicare ID card attached

Dear SUBROGATION REPRESENTATIVE,

Please be advised that I sustained injuries as a result of an accident that happened on the above date of loss. I am seeking damages from that accident from the tortfeasor (BI Insurance) or my first-party coverage (UM/UIM Insurance) or both.

It is my understanding that your company provided benefits to me in connection with accident-related treatment. Please provide me with an itemization of any and all benefits paid to me related to these injuries. For your convenience, I have enclosed a copy of my health insurance card.

Additionally, please advise if your company will be seeking reimbursement of any amounts paid for my benefit. If so, your company must, within thirty (30) days of receipt of this letter, provide me a statement asserting its payment of collateral source benefits and right of subrogation or reimbursement. An oral reply does not constitute compliance with this letter and does not fulfill your obligation(s) under the applicable State and Federal law(s).

If your company is asserting a right of subrogation or reimbursement, and if you comply with all legal requirements, I will contact you when the case is resolved.

The law requires that you cooperate with me by producing the information necessary for me to provide the nature and extent of the value of benefits provided. Your failure to cooperate may be taken into account by the Court in determining the right to, or the amount of, reimbursement asserted by your company.

To that end, it is requested that you provide the following:

1. A legible copy of any bills that have been presented to you which you have paid in whole or in part

2. A legible copy of any bills which have been presented to you, but which have not been paid

3. A legible copy of any medical reports from hospitals or physicians, or from any other source relied upon by you in any way in providing benefits

4. A true, legible copy of any contract or agreement supporting your claim to reimbursement or subrogation

5. A statement concerning the reason for nonpayment of any bills or the nonpayment of the full amount of any bills for which a claim has been made, referencing in each case the provisions of your contractor agreement which authorizes you to decline payment in whole or in part

It is requested that the above information is provided in a reasonable amount of time in response to this letter. At a later date, you may be asked to supplement your responses to the above-requested information based upon the events occurring after you have responded to this letter. The same information will be requested, and therefore, you are specifically requested to retain the necessary records to respond to the above questions when supplemental information is requested.

It is requested that the response be furnished to me by Certified Mail with Returned Receipt Service requested.

I have sent this notice because you may be a collateral source provider. By sending this letter, I am not admitting that you are a collateral source provider and that amount of any subrogation or reimbursement lien you may claim, and I retain the right to raise any defenses available to any claims by you for subrogation or reimbursement or if your company is asserting that these expenses were covered under an ERISA plan.

If you contend that the benefits paid on my behalf were provided under an employee welfare benefit plan covered by the Employee Retirement Income Security Act of 1974 (ERISA, 29 U.S.C. § 1001–1491), please forward the following documents and/or information to me within the next 30 days:

1. The Plan Document

2. The Summary Plan Description (SPD)

3. Form 5500 in effect as of the date of accident

4. If your company is not the Plan Administrator, then please identify the Plan Administrator and any plan or claim fiduciaries, including their addresses and phone numbers

5. A copy of each and every document related to the asserted subrogation claim in the possession of the Plan, the Plan Administrator, or any claim fiduciary which was used in determining that a subrogated interest exists (to include, but not limited to, your entire claim file(s), correspondence, medical records, bill, etc.)

6. A statement asserting whether or not the Plan is seeking subrogation, 100 percent reimbursement, or some other payback, or in the alternative, whether the Plan agrees that it is subject to the collateral source statute reference above

7. Please provide all bills, explanation of benefits (EOBs), or other documentation verifying such payment in your possession

A signed authorization to release information is enclosed for your records. Thank you for your time and prompt attention to this matter. If you have any questions or require additional information, please do not hesitate to contact me.

Sincerely,

_____

Your name, plaintiff
Address
City, State Zip
Cell Phone
Email Address

> **TRAUMATIC BRAIN INJURIES are extremely hard to diagnose. Most doctors miss them entirely. If you are checking yourself for a brain injury, you must do this checklist and then have your spouse, partner, or close friend also fill a clean copy out as well. Do not be surprised to find that your friends and family see a lot of issues you don't recognize in yourself.**

TRAUMATIC BRAIN/CLOSED HEAD INJURY CHECKLIST

The physical and cognitive symptoms described below can be associated with closed head injuries. Please note that numerous other symptoms may occur in more severe injuries or other types of brain injury, and this list is not an exhaustive one.

SYMPTOMS	PRESENT	ABSENT	EXPERIENCED IN THE PAST
✓ FRONTAL LOBE			
Loss of simple movement of various body parts (paralysis)			YES / NO
Difficulty multi-tasking or planning a sequence of complex movements			YES / NO
Loss of spontaneity			YES / NO
Loss of flexibility in thinking			YES / NO
Persistence of a single thought (perseveration)			YES / NO
Difficulty focusing on a task			YES / NO
Mood changes			YES / NO
Changes in personality			YES / NO
Difficulty with problem solving			YES / NO
Inability to express language (can't find the right words)			YES / NO

SYMPTOMS	PRESENT	ABSENT	EXPERIENCED IN THE PAST
✓ **PARIETAL LOBE**			
Difficulty attending to more than one object at a time			YES / NO
Difficulty naming objects			YES / NO
Difficulty reading			YES / NO
Difficulty drawing objects			YES / NO
Difficulty in distinguishing left from right			YES / NO
Difficulty with doing math			YES / NO
Difficulty to focus visual attention			YES / NO
Difficulty with eye and hand coordination			YES / NO
✓ **OCCIPITAL LOBE**			
Defects in vision (visual field cuts)			YES / NO
Difficulty with loading objects in the environment			YES / NO
Difficulty with identifying colors			YES / NO
Visual illusions–inaccurately seeing objects			YES / NO
Word blindness–inability to recognize words			YES / NO
Difficulty in recognizing and drawing objects			YES / NO
Difficulty with reading and writing			YES / NO

SYMPTOMS	PRESENT	ABSENT	EXPERIENCED IN THE PAST
✔ TEMPORAL LOBE			
Difficulty in recognizing faces			YES / NO
Difficulty in understanding spoken words			YES / NO
Difficulty with identification of, and verbalization about, objects			YES / NO
Short-term memory loss			YES / NO
Interference with long-term memory			YES / NO
Increased or decreased interest in sexual behavior			YES / NO
Difficulty in categorizing objects			YES / NO
Increased aggresive behavior			YES / NO
✔ BRAIN STEM			
Difficulty swallowing food & water			YES / NO
Difficulty with organization or perception of the environment			YES / NO
Problems with balance and movement			YES / NO
Dizziness and nausea			YES / NO
Sleeping difficulties			YES / NO
✔ CEREBELLUM			
Loss of ability to coordinate fine movements			YES / NO
Loss of ability to walk			YES / NO
Inability to reach out & grab objects			YES / NO
Tremors			YES / NO
Dizziness / Vertigo			YES / NO
Slurred speech			YES / NO
Inability to make rapid movements			YES / NO

APPENDIX H DEMAND LETTER FOR BI OR UM/UIM

This letter is the culmination of all the hard work over the past months, gathering evidence, getting witness statements, photos, and medical bills and treatment notes. You need to also have lifestyle stories here that will individualize this claim for your unique circumstance. There is no "right" way to do this letter, and you can be creative with it. However, this is the basic format for a typical Settlement Demand Letter.

Date

SENT VIA CERTIFIED MAIL #

INSURANCE COMPANY
Attention: ADJUSTER NAME
Address
City, State Zip

Re: Injured: *Name*
    Defendant: *Name*
    Claim No.: *Number*
    Date of Accident: *Date*
    Place of Accident: *Street name*

THIS LETTER IS A TIME-LIMITED DEMAND FOR SETTLEMENT

Dear ADJUSTER NAME:

My name is FULL NAME and I was involved in an automobile accident with Defendant on the above noted time and place. This accident was the sole negligence of the Defendant. I was not at fault.

This letter is my attempt to settle my claim against (If BI then "your insured", if UM/UIM then "my coverage") without involving the legal process of hiring lawyers. I expect to be treated as you would with any claim and that you will act in good faith dealing toward me as an unrepresented individual. I expect you to provide me the same settlement you would if I were represented. My goal is to provide you the information you need to properly settle this claim. This letter shall include all the information necessary to complete your review of my claim and provide me a fair settlement offer.

LIABILITY

On DATE OF ACCIDENT DEFENDANT'S NAME was driving direction on street.

(Describe here what the defendant did to cause the accident. Some of the most common causes are rear-end collisions, side impact accidents often called T-bone accidents, and any other situation where you believe the Defendant did something wrong and caused the accident. State what you believe happened in sufficient detail that the Adjuster will understand your complaint. However, do not be so detailed that you are locked into a position which may be unfavorable.)

(Describe what occurred after the wreck. Were the police called? Was the Defendant cited? Was an ambulance called? Was anyone arrested for DUI? Did you go to the hospital? Describe the property damage. Describe if you were feeling pain, what type of pain, and whether you are still in pain.)

INJURIES AND MEDICAL TREATMENT

Hospital evaluation: At the hospital the following occurred: (Describe what happened at the hospital).
Chiropractic evaluation
Orthopedic evaluation
Diagnostic testing (X-rays, CT Scans, MRI, Nerve Conduction Tests, Brain Injury Testing)
MMI/Impairment rating (If the doctor puts a medical impairment rating into your medical notes, add it here.)
Medical expenses (list all the medical bills)

LOST WAGE CLAIM AND OTHER ECONOMIC DAMAGES
OFFER TO SETTLE

The policy limits you disclosed to me indicate a limit of
For example: $10,000/$20,000, $25,000/$50,000, $50,000/$100,000, $100,000/$300,000, etc. The medical bills and economic damages total $ (Put in the total economic damages).

The noneconomic damages are significant.
I had the following troubles over the past months:
(Describe 2–5 stories on how badly you are hurting. Be brief but don't minimize the value of the pain or how it held you back.)

I believe my case is worth $ total.

I am offering a/an $ OFFER to settle this case today. (If your total damages are above the policy, you may not have an option if the insurance company failed to tender their limits to you at this time.)

Because the damages are above your insured's policy, I am offering to settle this matter for your insured's policy limits of the $ amount noted above.

It would be a mistake for your company not to pay the policy limits within the time limit. Any judgment, if I have to hire an attorney, will clearly exceed the policy limits.

This offer to settle is made in reliance upon your company's representation that the only coverage available is the amount of the policy limits previously provided in their correspondence to this office. If my understanding is correct regarding the policies governing your insured, we hereby offer to settle this matter for $ amount.

This offer will remain open until 1:00 p.m. TIME ZONE (EST, Central, Mountain). Please tender a check/draft made out to PLAINTIFF NAME to my house at Address, City, State, Zip.

This offer to settle is made subject to permission from my uninsured/ underinsured carrier. (Take this out if you are submitting this claim to UM/UIM carrier)

Thank you for your anticipated cooperation in working toward a mutually acceptable resolution of this matter.

Kindly be guided accordingly.

Sincerely,

_____

Your name, plaintiff
Address
City, State Zip
Cell Phone
Email Address

EXHIBITS ATTACHED
An example list of the exhibit you should include. MEDICAL RECORDS, POLICE REPORT, ECONOMIC DAMAGES

Exhibit "A" Accident Report
Exhibit "B" Hospital Records or Urgent Care
Exhibit "C" Chiropractor Records
Exhibit "D" Orthopedic Surgeon Records
Exhibit "E" Neurological Records
Exhibit "F" Brain Injury Psychologist
Exhibit "G" Diagnostic Testing (MRIs)
Exhibit "H" Diagnostic Testing (NCVs)
Exhibit "I" Witness Statement
Exhibit "J" Photographs

ABOUT THE AUTHOR

BRIAN LABOVICK is the CEO and founding partner at the LaBovick Law Group, a consumer justice law firm with the central business office in Palm Beach Gardens, Florida. The firm was founded in October 1991 in Miami, Florida. In 1994, it was relocated to Jupiter, Florida, where it flourished. Brian branded the firm as Warriors for Justice because this is the closest concept to how Brian feels he must handle his cases. Brian's mission is to maximize justice by aggressively fighting for his clients' rights. Brian graduated University of Miami School of Law as Order of the Barrister in 1990, passed the bar exam immediately, and was admitted to the Florida Bar a few months later. He is the former president of the North Palm Beach County Bar Association and former director of the Palm Beach County Justice Association. He has been named to the Top 100 Trial Lawyers list by the National Trial Lawyers Association, has a perfect 10/10 rating from AVVO, and holds an AV Preeminent Rating from Martindale-Hubbell. Brian is partners with Esther Uria LaBovick, his wife, who was a prosecutor for Janet Reno's State Attorney's Office in Dade County. They have three children and a dog named Leche.

DISCLAIMER

This book is not intended to be used as legal advice. It's intended to teach the process of what is necessary to settle an automobile accident claim.

The only way to fully protect yourself and maximize the value of any negligence claim is to hire a litigator. There is no short-cutting that fact. There is simply too much information to teach all of the aspects of negligence law in one short book.

That said, low-level injury cases are usually valued in a way that makes hiring an attorney unnecessary. The amount at risk is not significant enough for the injured person to hire an attorney. If you believe your injury is not significant enough to hire an attorney, you're welcome to use the lessons in this book to settle your own accident case. Just keep in mind that it is your judgment that is valuing your injury case. You're making the decision not to maximize that value but to save the expense of attorney's fees even though you will get a lesser total amount.